DANIEL JAY GROSSETT

Heaven or Hell

A True South London Story

This is a true story, but some names and identifying details have been changed to protect the privacy of the people involved.

First edition

This book was professionally typeset on Reedsy.
Find out more at reedsy.com

Mum, I hope I've made you proud

Natasha 'Tasha' Keifer, you will always remain in my heart, and I'll forever keep your spirit with me in all I do

And to you, dear reader, may good fortune follow you for all your life

Contents

Foreword

I am not perfect; who is? But within, I've detailed every aspect of my life as best possible. It contains things which may be hard to believe, but everything written is true. It may not be blemish free, but it's my best attempt to relay the extraordinary reality I experienced throughout my life. I hope you enjoy, it should enlighten you about a rarely explored world of events evolving up to the present, which we all influence. Please remember, **this is my 100% truth**.

1

Introduction

G od is great. So is the perfect, infinite truth. And life can be fantastic. This is my no-holds-barred, true story of growing up in south London, containing all the lessons I've learned. It's also a story about how I found heaven.

I hope my life story will provide a new perspective and a unique insight and outlook on life where nothing is impossible if we believe. Mistakes become lessons learnt. Lessons are blessings, and I've learned many. You can use these as a beneficial tool in your arsenal of knowledge, learn from my mistakes, and not make the same ones in your life.

There are many ways to improve life these days. There's nothing in this world we cannot achieve. We can do or be anything we want; that's the beauty of life. *I think, therefore, I am,* as the philosopher Descartes would say. Whatever we envision, what's stopping us from achieving that target but ourselves? I'm on my path to becoming a millionaire. Yes, a rich millionaire one day. Anything we can imagine is within our grasp. We're all affected by outside circumstances, but ultimately, our destiny is in our own hands.

My name is Daniel. Daniel, Jay, Grossett. Or, as I'm more well known, Duppy, the Jamaican word for ghost. This has been my nickname since the age of thirteen. I rarely use it now, but it seemed cool at the time and stuck with me throughout my life. I love my name. My initials are D.J.G.; I'm a D.J. who is a G. Ha. I loved music from a young age, and it runs in my family. Bob Marley is my second uncle, I believe. Mum said my uncle Gammospeng, a great D.J. and voiceover artist from Choice FM, has two children with Rita Marley's sister Miss P. That's the spiel I heard growing up, and Mum wasn't a liar, so who knows?

Choice FM was the biggest urban music radio station in the UK in the nineties and noughties. My uncle knew every yardie artist. I also bumped into Stormzy outside Blue Jays, the exclusive Caribbean food shop in South Norwood. All the top shottas went there for brunch. He was with my friend Ice, a real O.G. from the ends. Stormzy is probably the biggest rapper from south London.

I went from being the smartest kid in school with limitless potential getting the highest grades in my year to a needle-injecting heroin addict, having drug-induced psychotic episodes walking the streets of Brixton naked, committing crimes like shoplifting daily. I went in and out of prison for twelve years in a drug-fuelled destructive cycle. I spent half of that time inside, so I did roughly six years behind bars. I then changed my life, sobered up, and found what I call heaven.

When I speak of a world where I've found something that feels like heaven, I'm not talking about the place we hope to go after death. No, I'm a human being just like you and can only offer what is realistically possible. Only your creator can grant entrance there! I'm talking about fulfilling our destiny. Attaining a life so incredible, the only word to describe the sentiment is heaven.

Are you in? Do you want to find something to call heaven? Each journey is unique, but the destination is the same; we can all find heaven. But only *if* we want it. We must play our part, but that's the best bit. The adventure, the journey, the getting there. The part where we live, feel, and hopefully enjoy our emotions and experiences. We're needed one hundred percent. What's the other option? Let's call it the opposite for now. The opposing force. The no to our yes. Loss to our win. The never to our now. Nothing to our everything. Equal and opposites. Everybody has felt pain before; no sane being would choose it.

The opposite of my heaven is pain. We all face problems that anger us – that's life. It's how we deal with them that matters. It was almost hell, living how I didn't want to, without the ability, I thought, to change. Now life feels magical. I have begun a journey that would before seem nothing but a fantasy. I *have* found fulfilment wholeheartedly. I feel it every day. I've found heaven in my life, and this is a feeling we can all experience.

We can live any life we wish, within logic and reason. We can't just grow wings and fly, but that doesn't mean flying is impossible. Anything is possible. Man couldn't fly. Man built plane. Man flew! We can have anything we envision if we put our minds to it and give it our all. We're beings created from energy. What's truly stopping us? Nothing. It's a 'secret' few people know. Or believe, maybe?

This book is the true and tribulating story of how I became the content and happy person I am today. I wrote it as a record, guide, and inspiration for the future so we can be successful within and without. By without, I mean things outside the body and in the world around us, like becoming financially stable or getting a dream job. And we cannot forget the heaven part either - that's crucial. Heaven is what made me happy, successful, and will hopefully make me wealthy one day too.

As we go along this journey, you can hopefully learn something productive from my truth to experience it too. We are all on this journey there together. But it's up to you to write your destiny with your own hand and pen. No one else can write your path for you. You, Neo, must feel and experience the matrix for yourself. That's how you unlock your true power. You want to, need to, and can.

Blessings to one and all. Peace, as Prem Rawaat says. He created the Peace Education Course, which I completed in jail twice. I'll explain later. The story has just begun.

2

How It Started

I t all began back on the 17th of November 1987. I love my birth date. Perfection. Before birth, we were with the creator - infinity. There, we had a choice to be anything we could imagine or want to be in the possibilities of everything. If you start with nothing, the equal and opposite is everything. So, everything must be out there somewhere. I chose to be me. If I wanted to be something else, to feel or experience different energies, I would be in another part of the universe where I could live that expression.

Anyway, seventeen, eleven, nineteen eighty-seven. That day I felt like I'd won a race, which was great, but something felt missing. Life was missing. The part where I was alive, where I got to live out and sustain the urge to live. Fate brought me here, so this was my chance to fulfil it by finding true happiness. OK, I'll do my part one hundred percent. I am in!

I won. I won. I won the race! I was the sperm out of the millions that made it; luckily. I was alive. Thank God Almighty for that. I've wondered, what if a different sperm won? Would I be me? Wow. I was lucky. Millions! Lucky is not the word. My parents had created me, and that was the main thing.

My earliest memories are a slight feeling of winning that race, which is crazy because I was a sperm. I felt like I had raced with my all. My first tangible memory is being in a cot in a red room with my mum. It's faint now but a memory, nonetheless. I remember many early experiences, primarily with Mum listening to music or using a hairdryer. And being in a cot. Those first experiences were a treasure. They are dear memories.

It must have been 1988, and the next thing I remember is playing on a bed with my mum and brother. My older brother's name is Damon. He is currently in a mental institution for stabbing a man after going a bit psycho. But all that comes later. I next remember becoming more aware. I wasn't fully self-aware, but I had a big brother who was the best in the world to me. He had my back from birth. Mum said he'd pick me up and bring me over to her when I was little; I love him dearly.

Mum would pretend to be dead on the bed. We'd fly into a panic until she spooked us with a boo. Damon is only eighteen months older than me, so we grew up together. This is something I'd recommend when considering children. If you want them, give your children siblings close in age to grow together. To me, it mattered. My big brother loved me and proved it every day. Before birth, I remember a feeling of peace, darkness, and stillness forever. Before our incarnation, we were all together with God. But that was over because I was alive.

Sunlight is spectacular when first seen. Those young memories were beautiful moments I wouldn't replace for the world. They were precious indeed. Enthralling times at Brighton beach with flashing fairground lights. Exotic magical experiences. Luckily, I had Damon, who guided and taught me everything he knew.

I became more aware around age three when I started nursery at Christ Church Primary school in Battersea. We did finger painting, sang the alphabet, and got a milk carton daily. I've stolen milk from kids' schools as an adult. It's terrible, but it's the reality of my previous ways. We played a game where we threw a stone from up high, and you won by retrieving it first where it landed. One day, I threw it from the top of the climbing frame and hit my friend George straight in the face. He burst into tears, and I ran to say sorry, but the teacher's face said it all. This wasn't good. He was hurt. I got in trouble, and it scarred him. I learned of a bad outcome. I discovered conditions I didn't like finding myself in - that's for sure. That and getting dead legs when hitting them in the playground. I recall nursery like yesterday. At home, we also luckily owned a computer console, the Atari. It had little graphical power compared with today's tech, but it was the latest console.

I soon moved up to reception year, started flute lessons, and had great fun playing with friends. Around four years old, we hung up our jackets when coming in from the rain and learned exciting new things. Enthralling new smells, tastes, sights, and sounds. And there was one thing more special than anything else. A beacon of light in my life who was always there for me. My starlight and my sunshine, my dear mother.

My mum was my best friend, God rest her soul. She passed away from cancer in 2020, which was the worst thing I'd ever experienced. She is in Heaven now with God. When I talk of heaven in this book, it's as real to me as the Heaven where I believe my mother is. I remember her vividly. She was always there for me and was the strength of my life. I didn't truly know myself, but I knew Mum. Her name is Louise Mary Willison, and she was *the one.*

We had dreamy times in Eastbourne at Nan's during the holidays. Nan would tuck us into bed with a glass of milk and some biscuits, followed by a big sloppy kiss we'd unsuccessfully avoid. We had car journeys where I threw up. Aunty Janet told us to eat ginger biscuits which took away the sickness. Exciting adventures in the garden with cousins and all the joys of being a kid. I have fantastic memories, as you may also have yourself. Because you aren't much different to me, we simply live from different perspectives.

We all come from one thing: the original seed. A seed grows into a tree and then has seeds of its own, which spread fruit and more seed themselves, multiplying forever. Even when there are zillions of trees, they all stem from that original seed. Some may call it the primordial fireball. I call it God.

I have many memories as a young child that felt spectacular indeed. You hopefully experienced something similar if you were lucky enough to have a great childhood. Those days were my first, so they were extraordinary. Visiting the seaside as a baby was a great memory for me. Did you have any childhood holidays? Heavenly, were they not? Treasure your memories, for they are priceless jewels.

Before five years old, I wasn't fully self-aware yet; I was learning. Learning what was right and wrong, just like you. We can all sense right from wrong. Being self-aware is like *The Terminator* movie, we are like artificial intelligence. We become self-aware of ourselves, do we not? We didn't create ourselves, yet we can create. We can make whatever we want every day when we choose what we do.

Whatever you realise in the present, you create it into existence, like me making this book. Or creating children. From created to the creator. Equal and opposite. All things have equal and opposite; it's a law of nature. All things except God. God created this law and is therefore not subjugated by it. God is all things, the original one, and has no opposite. I'm not saying God from a religious perspective; I mean the energy that created all.

Every action has an equal and opposite reaction. This law governs all things in existence, even your thoughts. So, be careful what you think because every vibration you create resonates all around you. We, humans, are self-aware, intelligent supreme beings. In essence, we're someone else's artificial intelligence. We're intelligent and didn't create ourselves, that's for sure.

We all have special memories as children. Not all, actually, because not everyone had such endearing experiences. There are evil people in this world and some have kids. Innocent children have suffered unimaginable pain. So, if you were lucky enough to have a pleasant upbringing, please count your blessings; things could always be worse. Society can forget that life was more challenging in the past. There's more wealth on earth than ever, yet people are still without clean drinking water. If you knew how beneficial a positive outlook on life can be, I'm sure you'd try to stay as positive as possible.

Those childhood days were heavenly. This might shock you, but those days are worth a fraction of today's value. The days you live now hold more potential than all your previous ones. Because right now, you're in the present. The present contains all you are from your whole life experience, plus the infinite potential of the moment. There are a million ways your life could go right now, and all that potential is owned by you. With your freedom of choice, you're fully in control. You are where you are and doing what you're doing because you chose, are you not? You are a functioning human who controls your actions and hopefully understands that your choices affect your reality.

Today is limitless. It may seem hard to swallow, but to some degree, it's true. I'm not trying to diminish your memories; they were all perfect in their own perfection. But all your past encounters prepared you for the present, which is your most significant moment. Eckhart Tolle wrote in *The Power of Now* that now is your strongest. You can't get better. Why? You are now vibrating at your highest possible vibration. As you grow and learn daily, you adjust yourself to be your most refined version. And because now is the latest the universe offers, where it presents itself to you as a present, do appreciate its presence.

It's also because you could possibly lose right now at any moment. Yes, life is precious and shouldn't be taken for granted. It could be taken away in the blink of an eye. One day it will be gone; that's promised from birth. You were nothing, and now you're alive. But your physical body will die, and it'll return to nothing. Your life experience is what you take with you to the next realm. If you do evil in this life, you reap it multiplied infinitely in the next. That's your seed growing into a tree. Do good, and it's the same, multiplied infinitely. That's the beauty of life; whatever seeds we plant will multiply forever. So plant good seeds, you'll eat the fruit of those trees. You never know when it's your time to go, so the present is always precious.

Life was a matter of survival until civilization became more sophisticated. We now live in flourishing times. Yet, as sweet as life is in prosperous countries, there is still war, suffering, and innocent people dying. So please appreciate the luxuries that have come to be the norm. If the least of those were missing, you'd notice immediately. Now is precious and contains enough treasure to keep you hunting forever.

If you have children, you may relate to how precious today is because kids are only that age once. You're still that child inside yourself, as your experiences and childhood memories will forever be part of you. But now you're the care provider to that child too. You are both. Whether you're a parent or not, you are still the primary care provider to yourself. It's your job to be there for yourself when needed. From sufficiently eating to staying healthy and surviving down to having an emotional outlet where you can functionally have a sacred moment like you did as a child. Yep, both.

Your emotional health is just as important as your physical. When your emotional health thrives, you'll notice the benefits physically also. It's your job to make sure all those things go smoothly. It's not that hard; you're not alone. You always have the creator with you. God is inside and all around you. You also have the strength of your predecessors, such as your parents. All their positive energy is within you. Don't worry; you'll be fine. You'll prosper if you align yourself with truth, love, and do good. This is because the universe gives you what you seek from it. That's the 'secret' I learned from the great author Rhonda Byrne, who wrote an incredible book about it, which we'll delve into later.

3

Early Days

I loved learning at school; it was my favourite thing. It was unlimited how much you could learn. Like numbers, once you start counting, you can keep counting forever! I fell deeper in love with computer games and all the excitement they brought. We had a Sega Master System with the latest technological advancement, *Alex the Kidd* built in. How times have changed. Imagine the advances we'll make in the future. We also got a kitten and named her Nightshade after the Gladiator from the nineties' television show *Gladiators*.

Michael Jackson inspired us. His music, his dance moves, his movie *Moonwalker*. We loved it all, as did everyone. He was a significant influence, and we had the curls to match. I met new cousins and had adventurous fairy-tale summers filled with exciting new experiences. We all grew up together, learning new things every day. We had Easter egg hunts, built tree houses, played in the mud, and did various physical activities. Nowadays, technology has changed how children grow as they're more inclined to play with computers than physical play, but we had no choice back then. My parents blessed me with a beautiful childhood. Thinking back on it makes me smile. God bless mothers and fathers who raise children with all their love.

It was the September of 1992 when two months before my fifth birthday I became the proud big brother to a baby boy named Alex. How can I forget to mention my dad, Clive Hayles? I don't share the same surname as this legend of a man. This is because he's not Damon and my biological father. We didn't know this at the time as he was noble and had raised us since we were toddlers. I love him dearly because he treated us as his own, and we got to experience all the joys of having a loving father. He was my dad, and I'll love him forever.

Even as a grown man now, I've contemplated the integrity of taking on a lady with two toddlers, so I sincerely admire my dad and others like him. A good honest, hard-working person. A strength to society. He was Alex's father, though, and as newborns do, Alex took centre stage for a while. That never bothered me; it was an intriguing experience that I cherished.

We were living in Battersea, and life was sweet. The demanding school routine dominated. However, we regularly visited family on weekends and school holidays, a beautiful mix of English and Jamaican heritage. Two hugely different cultures, yet both were equally treasured. We'd visit Grandma on my dad's side and have delicious Caribbean food that makes me hungry at the thought. Jerk chicken, rice and peas, dumplings, and plantain. These were genuine loving family moments. We had family feasts and played Monopoly after. Our cool Aunty Lorraine was a bit younger than Dad, and everyone showered us with hugs and kisses.

We also visited Nan from Mum's side for sensational English Sunday roasts. Yorkshire puddings, lamb, mint sauce, and all. We had it good indeed, experiencing the best of both worlds. We loved it also because Mum's younger brother, Uncle Paul, had a Super Nintendo with *Super Street Fighter 2 Turbo*. This kept us going for hours, and most of my generation knows how legendary that game is.

We had thrilling adventures playing with our cousin Hayley. We met Mum's cousins Katy and Gary, who were closer to our age than hers. Mum's lovely best friend from school, Dawn, sometimes visited. Mum told us she and Dawn had leather jackets long enough to nearly touch the floor back in their day, with the most notable splits up the back to show they were the coolest. Funny how fashion changes over time.

I soon experienced my first kiss; her name was Jessica; she was a little blonde girl in my class at school. I felt ecstatic when we kissed on the playground; my body tingled. We had assemblies in the dining hall that the entire school attended. We all sat on the floor singing hymns from words displayed on a projector. It strengthened my memory because I soon knew every song.

I experienced something in my childhood that only certain people can relate to. BEATINGS! We got spanked if we were naughty, and the belt was used if we were very bad. Dad would only have to say, 'Right, time for the belt,' and we'd sprint in all directions, running upstairs and hiding under beds. I farted intentionally on my dad's hand when he smacked me once. I thought, oh no, I've got him angrier, but luckily, he didn't make too much of it. That one made us laugh.

He was a great father and only punished us when we deserved it. I thank my dad for those beatings because knowing I'd get a spank kept me from being naughty. I logically understood that being bad was not worth the smack. It was less beneficial, so I behaved. When I did experience a beating, it was the most physical pain I'd ever felt. I was lucky to not experience much discomfort from external sources. So, I did the math. Worse pain ever versus being good; I chose to be good.

I'm not condoning beating, but children lack wisdom and experience, so parents must raise them properly with respect, dignity, and manners. If you let the child be in control, it benefits nobody. That's like having surgery done by someone without any medical training. They lack the knowledge to get the task completed correctly. Raise children compassionately but remember that the parent is the caregiver. It's their responsibility to instil discipline. This doesn't mean physically hitting a child. It means teaching them right from wrong and ensuring they implement and adhere to that knowledge. Children depend on their parents for guidance and subconsciously prefer correction, even if it's not what they want to hear. We can also offer our children the life we wanted or never had.

Our kitten, Nightshade, soon matured and had kittens of her own. We kept the one with the black spot on his nose and named him Bruno, after the British boxing champion, Frank Bruno. He was my little best friend and slept under the covers with me; we were inseparable. Around this time, Mum took all three of us to do some modelling pictures. We got spruced up, put our best clothes on, and gelled our hair. It was a lovely day out, a new adventure.

Everything is new when you're young. The world was my oyster, and I could be anything I wanted. That was something my parents instilled in me throughout my youth. I was unsure what I wanted to be, but I knew one thing: I wanted to be great. To be the best, better than everything there ever was. I knew that whatever I was going to be, it had to be greater than the greatest up till that point. If I could achieve it, I'd be happy. That meant being better than Michael Jackson, in my eyes. How would I do it? He was the best. I was unsure but knew it was the only way to fulfil my desire and potential.

The Fibonacci sequence expresses the current being more significant than the previous, and I wanted exactly that. The Fibonacci sequence is the mathematical design of the universe. Almost all known physical things are designed through it, including the human body and the galaxies. It follows a number pattern of growth with the numbers 0,1,1,2,3,5,8,13,21,34,55, and so forth, adding the previous two together to create a single, more significant counterpart. It makes perfect sense that the universe is designed this way; it is a perfect growth pattern.

So, not knowing my life direction, I simply tried my best. And it was working. Because I was soon first in class and getting great school reports. I was that lucky kid who was the smartest. All the way from reception at around five years old to age thirteen. Talking of luck, here is one for unlucky. Or unwise, I should say. Once, I decided to get a piece of polystyrene and scrape it along the brick walls of every house on my street. I thought, yay, look how much mess I can make, hoping the wind would blow it away. But nope, Dad found out speedily, and the wind didn't blow it away, not quick enough, anyway. So he made me sweep the whole street clean.

My father disciplined us correctly, adamantly teaching us right from wrong. We knew the consequences of bad decisions. Fearing punishment kept us on the straight and narrow. But that was the sweet way out, much better than the belt. Our dad was strict but good to us; we heard stories from second cousins of stringent parents. But yes, I was first in class, and it became simple: one plus one makes two. What else do you need to know? Once you know that, you can work out anything if you try, right? That's how it was for me, and I ensured I was the best at it.

I stuck to being the best at one plus one makes two, and before long, I kept succeeding. I tried until I completed the task, propelling me upwards. The more I learned, the easier it got. Because even the most frustrating of equations still come from our one creator. Nothing is impossible with God because all things come from one. And for me, life was as simple as one plus one makes two.

Another major thing during childhood was television; it hugely affected my life. *Hook*, the Peter Pan movie, powerfully influenced me. We kids had an unspoken pact. We believed we were like Pan and would never grow up. I've kept that principle to a degree because I feel a part of me will forever be that inner child. But now, as a man, I take pride in my maturity. It's up to you to make the right decisions in your life; as you grow, you'll learn to make more right decisions. Aren't these the foundations of a modest adult? If you're getting things right, you aren't getting them wrong. And getting things correct is the backbone of adulthood. Making the right decisions at the right time. I've learned this while maturing through life.

4

Battersea/Primary School Days

School life was spectacular; everything was perfect. Slowly growing up, life couldn't have been sweeter. We weren't rich but had enough and never went without. We jumped for joy when Dad came home from work and regularly surprised us with computer games. *FIFA 93* was the latest. Routine was everything. Wake up, go to school, come home, and snack. Then watch *Nickelodeon* or play outside.

Once Mum told her friend Trisha, who lived across the road with six children, about a surprise she'd planned. Her youngest son Jamie, the naughty one, overheard and took pleasure in spoiling it. Our first visit to the cinema and Wimpy's for a burger afterwards. No longer a surprise, we still had a fantastic day out. Watching *The Mask*, starring Jim Carrey, on a massive screen with surround sound was thrilling.

Mum's best friend, Aunt Mandy, had a cool son, Leigh. He'd bring his computer games around, and we'd battle away while our mums gossiped with cigarettes and tea. Now might be different, but when we'd grown up with someone close from a young age, we half considered them family. The internet has connected the world, so social bubbles are larger nowadays. But back then, it was mostly in person if you wanted to see or speak to someone. Phones were around but were used nowhere near as much as now. We'd watch *Nickelodeon* all day.

Summer holidays came, and we had exciting new adventures for six weeks, dreading our return to school. We'd get the most out of every day, especially the sunny ones. Beautiful summer days, having picnics at Battersea Park. Food, drink, and rounders brought hours of fun. Mum took Alex on the swings while we played football. Dad was great. The love we felt from both our parents was exquisite. Those days were heavenly and are treasured memories indeed.

The good thing about the return to school meant it'd soon be winter, and winter brought Christmas. They were magical experiences filled with awe, love, and joy. We'd eat one chocolate a day from the advent calendar, sometimes nicking two. We'd wake up early, dash into our parent's bedroom, and jump on the bed, hollering, 'It's Christmas. Mum, Dad, wake up.' We would race downstairs to our spectacular glowing tree and start lining our presents up. Alex was a toddler, so we'd help him with his; smallest first, saving the biggest and best until last.

Alex grew fast. He was huge, like his uncle Michael, a basketball player for the Thames Valley Tigers. He went on to coach them and opened his own sports shop, *Sir Sports*. But yes, Alex was a diamond, and he sponged up love from us all. Maybe he grew up fast because he had two big brothers to learn from. Homelife was sweet, and I thrived at school.

In year one, I had a few main friends: the most popular kids, Samir, Phillip, and Tyrone. I clicked with them as we were all protagonists in life's story. Tyrone was probably my bestie as he was quiet and reserved. That's why I liked him; he was humble. These were the days of the original Nintendo Gameboy and the first mobile phones when they had ten numbers instead of eleven. I still remember my dad's first number, 0958276004. My memory is crazy like that. Nowadays, mid-conversation, I'll completely forget what I'm saying. It happens regularly and is frustrating, but I remember my past vividly.

Dad was immensely proud when he got his new work van with his company details on the side. Soon Alex ballooned in size and could keep up with us older brothers. So, we officially became a threesome. When Alex was two, I was seven, and Damon was eight. Our uncle, Michael and Aunty Jane took our families to Alton Towers one summer day; boy, was that fun. We loved the rides, especially the scary ones. My favourite was the Ghost Trains, the fast ones, and the ones you go up high. The thought alone makes me want to plan a future trip right now!

There was never a dull moment in our house, always something exciting to do. We'd play fight, and Alex would dive right into the action; he loved it. Later in life, he became a bouncer; it figures. We luckily got a Sega Mega-drive one Christmas. An upgrade from the 8-bit graphics of the Sega Master System to the 16-bit Mega-Drive. It was the latest and greatest then, but in comparison, now the basic smartphone is way more advanced.

We'd visit our cousins, Lewis' and Lauren's house and play *Sonic and Tails* until our fingers ached. *Sonic* was the main title for Sega, while *Super Mario* was its primary competitor on Nintendo. It's a bit like the battle between PlayStation and X-Box nowadays. We were Sega kids; *Sonic* brought us hours of joy.

Throughout these experiences, I felt nothing but love from my light and shining star, my dear mum. She was perfect in every way. A role model. She set the bar high, so for any girl to compete, they would need to be special. Looking back, I wouldn't change a thing about Mum. Nor the experiences and memories we shared. That's a powerful energy, something you'd never change. She instilled the utmost love and affection into us all. We weren't rich in money but were billionaires in love.

Another massive influence on our upbringing was movies from America. The internet was in its infancy, so the latest trends came from what we saw around us and on television. Nineties Hollywood movies inspired us to dream to the stars. We admired the older kids and aspired to adventure just like them. That's how society works. First, the younger generation admires the current and aspires to its greatness; then, they improve upon it in their lifetime. They become more remarkable than the previous generation; thus, setting a higher standard for the next. Then the next generation repeats and continues the cycle.

Balance is the key to life. All things are in balance; otherwise, they'd be unstable. You cannot have left without right, up without down. There's no yin without yang or black without white. But there is also a broad spectrum of colours in between. Just as there're many angles in between right and left, down and up, life is the same. There are infinite different outcomes that we can influence and control. Every thought, word, and action you make in your life will affect its path. You may think your activities are secret; they are in one essence. But the universe feels our every vibration and rewards us accordingly.

Back then, the world was a lot more racist than nowadays. The earth has only recently become sophisticated and is improving every day. But the further you go back, the more uncivil and barbaric humanity was. The nineties were more unsophisticated than nowadays. And the sixties were more uncivilised than the nineties, and so forth. People did a lot of evil in the past because they could get away with it. Many people in jail with life sentences are never getting out. Society has improved, so consider yourself lucky. In my eyes, I was the luckiest boy in the world - always having fun. I could do anything I wanted with life and be anything imaginable. I could write the unwritten future however I wished.

We had a smooth routine of school and playtime. Dad took Damon and me for an incredible day of go-karting. They went so fast that Dad helped me drive. We raced, us versus Damon; we luckily won. We also went to fairgrounds, spinning in teacups and bumping in bumper cars, leaving with a giant sweet red dummy or candy floss. The good old days.

We'd go to Gaulden Park, a fenced concrete football pitch only a three-minute walk from our house and play football with the older boys. Damon always had my back, no matter the situation. We went everywhere together, with Mum regularly dressing us identically. We disliked it sometimes, looking like twins, but I admire my mum for it now.

One day at the park, I got into a fight. An older boy tried to bully me off the swing. I stood up to him, but he punched me and my nose bled. Damon didn't get involved because it was a one-on-one; we kept our principles, despite his advantage. I took my loss and made the walk of shame back home. The drama queen I was made sure I got as much blood as possible over my t-shirt, hoping the shock would initiate some help from Dad. It worked! Dad got vexed, cleaned me up, and stormed us back to the park to find this 'older' boy. When we arrived, Dad saw he was only slightly older and realised he could do nothing. We walked back home a little deflated, but Dad reassured me everything would be OK.

'Don't worry, son; next time, you'll get the win.' I learned that day that acting got me nowhere. I knew getting blood all over myself was wrong, but I did it for attention. I never made that mistake again, so it became a lesson well learnt.

Jamal, a kind boy one year older than Damon, lived a few doors down our street. We admired him. He was light-skinned black, and in a majority-white, slightly racist area, he looked out for us. He had a little sister, Alex's age.

Mum was on benefits but had a secret part-time job in the local delicatessen at the top of our road. A school friend knew this and threatened to tattletale one time we had argued. Mum babysat his little brother, so I knew something un-great about him. I thought, should I tell? But I knew it was a nasty thing to do deep down, so I tried the other path, saying nothing. It all worked out smoothly. That day I discovered things can be resolved better if you don't react in anger. An angry reaction differs from an appropriate one. They resonate at different frequencies, so they have alternative effects and outcomes.

Our next-door neighbour was known as pigeon chest Pete. We also had a friend called James, who lived close by. He had an older sister named Laura, and their mum was an alcoholic, but she was kind. We once saw her fall out of their ground-floor front room window. She got straight up and said something like, 'Fuck you, you're a cunt,' and walked off like it was nothing. James was notoriously the strongest under eleven-year-old in Battersea. Jimmy White, the snooker legend, was his godfather; I saw pictures of them together.

We knew another Laura too, who lived across the road with her five siblings. She'd visit us and play blind date, kissing under the bed. The local bully was a tomboy named Becky, whose reputation for beating up boys preceded her. Our childhood was any kid's dream, like a fairy tale.

We played kiss chase at school, trying to catch the pretty girls and avoid the scary ones. I was still the smartest in class and got the top results. But a lovely African girl, Suru, was challenging me for my spot. She was just as innovative as me and kept me on my toes. Healthy competition is fantastic fuel for success. I loved watching *Ally McBeal* and wanted to be a lawyer one day; everyone said I was smart enough. Alex was three but was a little warrior, enormous for his age.

Dad sometimes took me to his friend, Uncle Terry, who had a fully built recording studio in his bedroom. I sang on a beat he made for me; it was wicked. I was like seven and had my own little song. The words were from a 'true story' one of my teachers taught us at school. She said there were prisoners of war in another country who were marched outside into the snow with no clothes. Their feet got stuck to the ice, and people died. So they sang a song to keep themselves warm and alive. That song was, 'All I ask of you is forever to remember me, as loving you.' And that was all I could think of, so that was my first song.

Sega-Saturn and PlayStation had just come out. The graphics are laughable now, but they were state-of-the-art back then. Remember, even the wheel was the latest technology once. One Christmas, we got our first mountain bikes, which took us a while to master, with a few crashes on the way. We also got our first pair of Nike trainers. Oh boy, that meant a lot to us. We wanted for nothing but weren't rich, so we didn't have many designer clothes. We were well-loved and always looked tidy, but like many, our parents weren't willing to pay a fortune just for the latest fashion. So, our first Nikes were treasured.

You wouldn't believe what Damon did with his. After changing into rollerblades, he left them in a bag outside the local sweet shop. He forgot it as we walked home, literally two weeks after getting them. We ran back, but they were gone. He was disheartened, but there was always something sweet about life. We had great parents who couldn't have raised us better. Life was a dream. Once again, I wouldn't change this period in my life for the world. But my world soon changed. Alex was getting big, so the two-bedroom house in Battersea was no longer sufficient. So off to Kennington we went.

5

Kennington

We moved to Kennington around 1996, not far from Battersea. Our school was within walking distance before, but now we had to take the bus. I was about eight at the time, Damon was ten, and Alex was three, although he was the size of a five-year-old. We'd play fight, and even though I was older, he always gave me a good challenge. Once, I slightly abused my advantage when Alex was getting the upper hand. He caught me with a good punch, unintentionally hitting my eye. I retaliated angrily, punching him in rage. He burst into tears, and I felt terrible. I immediately hugged him, 'Alex, I'm sorry.' He was a little gangster, and he took it like a man. When we made peace, I vowed never to do anything like that again. Alex wiped away his tears and carried onwards and upwards.

Our new house was incredible, it had an extra bedroom and a more extensive garden. One summer, Alex came running inside screaming, 'There's an octopus. There's an octopus outside!' Damon and I rushed into the garden, and to our surprise, there was a dead mouse on the grass. We burst out laughing. Life was like a box of chocolates, full of surprises

I was alive in the present, which has infinite potential. This meant I could be anything I wished to be and even better than all before me. Maybe I *could* be more significant than Michael Jackson - why not? Learn from the best and become greater; that was my motto. Everything made sense. I was doing incredibly well in school, especially in math. I was way ahead, and it seemed easy to understand, so the sky was the limit.

Life was beautiful, and beauty is in the eye of the beholder. Yes, one person's love could be another person's hate. Maybe it's all down to perception because to me, life was perfect. Perception is our unique view of life, and we all perceive life to our level of understanding. Imagine a millionaire loses all his millions and is left with only ten thousand pounds. He feels terribly distraught. On the flip side, a homeless man has just been gifted ten thousand pounds and he's over the moon. Both have the same money, but their feelings towards it are incredibly different. These emotions all stem from their perception.

A positive mental attitude is always beneficial. The glass is half full rather than half empty. The drink in that glass tastes sweeter. Life is what you make it. Do you know the power of your choice? Your choice is infinite, just like your imagination. Think about it: what limits your choice or imagination? Nothing except yourself. Within your freedom of choice, you hold immense power. You can think whatever you want, without limitation. If we lose our choice, we lose our freedom.

Our thoughts are limited only by what we perceive is possible through our physical bodies. Really, your body is only limited by what your spirit believes is possible. You're a spirit, living an experience through your body. It has the correct senses to perceive everything you need to fulfil your spirit's wants. That's why you're here on earth: to fulfil your emotional and spiritual destiny. And you are in your physical body to achieve it. You can create any future you want. You have the power to manifest any reality you desire.

Don't be disillusioned into believing you *are* your physical body. It's just a vehicle for your soul. The perfect companion for your spirit to fulfil its will. Imagine your spirit as the computer software and your body as the software's laptop. It needs the computer hardware to work through, but they are separate entities collaborating. Your spirit connects you with your limitless choice and imagination. And your spirit is your direct connection with the creator. While alive, you have a genuine relationship with the creator of your software. Meaning you can upgrade and improve your software while inside that hardware.

When incarnated in a physical body, your spirit can grow infinitely. And your soul is what you take into the next life beyond the physical. So, utilise your opportunity now whilst alive to grow into whom you want to be. This life is your only chance, and love is the key.

Mum's smile always saved the day. She took us to school on the bus, going through Vauxhall and past Battersea Power Station and Dog's Home. We soon got back into a routine. We attended many family dos, like christenings and weddings. These were thrilling events, constantly meeting new cousins. Our Aunty Mavis named all her children's first names with 'M': Marlon, Melvin, and Miguel.

At these gatherings, the grownups sometimes acted funny. In hindsight, I realised this was due to alcohol consumption. I tried beer; it tasted disgusting. One time there was a big commotion at a christening afterparty. We ran to see what was happening. Mum had got into a fight! No one was hurt, but trouble sometimes gravitated toward her at these events. I later understood this was because my mum wasn't an excellent drinker. She had a heart of gold but got a bit carried away when she had one too many. Mum was militant like a soldier and could hold down her liquor, but she was only human.

We had night-time adventures with various cousins while our parents slow-danced to old reggae. The sweet scent of alcohol and cigarette smoke fogged the air. A fragrance that only lives in myth since you can no longer legally smoke inside public places. But back then, that smell was prominent at almost any social event, and anyone old enough will remember its dominance. Everybody danced, seamlessly happy, living life. Kennington was great.

Christmas of '97, we got a Nintendo 64. It'd been available for a while, so it had dropped in price. Dad liked computers, so we always eventually got the latest consoles. This brought a whole new experience because up until then, computers mainly supported two players only. This one supported four, which was great because everyone could play. It came with the incredible *Goldeneye 007*, and even Mum gave it a go. We battled for hours, Alex sometimes crying because we rapidly beat him. The graphics were three-dimensional and way more advanced than our Sega Mega-drive. I'd briefly played on a PlayStation at my friend's and Uncle Paul's, but now we owned our own N64; man, we were in the game.

But Mum and Dad soon started arguing more often, mostly at night. Things sometimes turned sour after alcohol. They'd try to not disturb us, but neither backed down, so it could get heated. These arguments were non-violent, but Mum sometimes got physical.

We never knew then how much our life would soon change. Their arguing finally got the better of them and Dad moved out. He said goodbye, crying. I thought, wow, is this really happening? It was emotional, but I never knew what to feel. We said goodbye watching him walk out the door. This was major, but I couldn't comprehend its true impact. Dad was gone, leaving just me, Mum, Damon, and Alex.

6

The Cracks Start To Appear

Mum was left to raise us all on her own. She must've been around thirty-three. Wow, a single mother with three children - salutes don't pay homage. Alex attended nursery at Henry Fawcett Primary School. It was near Kennington Oval cricket grounds, so Mum would take us all to drop Alex off and then take Damon and me on the bus to school. We did this for a while, and Mum did it gracefully. I mean, no one's perfect, but Mum gave her all. She held it down so well that things never changed much. Kudos to her.

That year Damon left me behind in primary school, heading into secondary. We knew we might get away with more mischief without Dad around, but we weren't so inclined. We loved and missed him dearly. We'd no longer play football or computer games together. He had cleaned us when we messed up the bed. He taught us how to stand up for ourselves - how'd we survive without him? We weren't sure, but we had to make the best of the current situation. Luckily, Mum ran things smoothly, ensuring we weren't affected much.

We discovered the most incredible 'football pitch' twenty metres from our house that summer. We lived on Courtenay Street, and it had a little grass area near ours. Trees were conveniently positioned for goalposts, perfect for footy. We played outside for hours, only stopping when Mum shouted, 'Damon, Dan, Alex. Dinner's ready.' We'd battle between scoring one more goal and getting inside before our food went cold, trying to finish as quickly as possible. That one more goal often turned into three until Mum hollered, 'Right, it's your last warning; if you don't hurry up, it's going in the bin!' Then we'd all run inside to a delicious plate of food. You can't beat a mum's cooking, can you?

Life was sweeter than a kiss from a rose. But Mum started becoming what we called 'woo' at night. Slurring words and acting funny, a little tipsy or drunk. It was noticeable sometimes, but she held it down well. We didn't know many people locally because we still went to school in Battersea. But in year five, Mum switched my school to one closer. She tried to get me into the same one as Alex, but it wasn't possible halfway through the school year. So, Mum enrolled me at Vauxhall Primary School.

This was exciting, and I quickly made new friends. I was on Heinemann's mathematics book level eight. The highest book they had in my class was level two. I was even ahead of the kids in the year above, so far ahead that they didn't have my level book in the school; they ordered it just for me. That was an ego boost, for sure. But school life here was too simple. We were ten, playing with Lego half the day. It got boring, so I pushed and challenged myself. It was fun, though.

We'd play sting ball in the P.E. hall, trying to hit people as hard and fast as possible with a softball. I also learned chess, which we played almost every day. I was excellent, as were a few others. It showed they had great potential. It never took long to start shining here because I soon got the leading role in the Christmas play. I performed as Scrooge in *A Christmas Carol*, with Mum watching from the audience. I got almost every word right, with only one little mistake. I was proud because it showed my determination.

We slowly befriended the kids on our street, and there were loads of us. Tom and his sister across the road were both quiet. Peter and Murphy lived a few doors down; their mum became good friends with ours. Kelvin, Delvin, and Vanessa lived even closer. And Reece and Liam lived down at the end. They were all our age and only a minute away; it couldn't have worked out better. We also had Charlotte and Gemma, our two female companions.

Charlotte was Alex's age, and we teased him, calling her his girlfriend. And

Gemma. Oh, she was probably my first proper crush. She was one year older than Damon and gorgeous. Like the girl next door mixed with your high school sweetheart. She knocked on my door once, 'Hi Louise, is Daniel allowed out?' Asking for me gave me butterflies. Wow, I thought she wanted to see Damon. All the girls fancied him growing up; they went crazy for his green eyes. But this time, she asked for me.

Alex played with Charlotte while we hung out with Gemma. We debated who she liked between Damon and Peter as they were her age. But being young, they were both a bit shy about anything serious. Even though she was only fourteen, Gemma was way ahead in her adolescence. She hung around with sixteen-year-old boys and wasn't a virgin. Growing up, I heard that girls mature a little faster than boys; it might be true. She definitely was something to dream about.

Things soon started to change because Mum became 'woo' more often; she drank almost every day. Of course, she wasn't always drunk, but a day passing without her having at least one beer was rare. She got drunk sometimes but managed to hold everything down like a great mother. She'd be perfectly normal, then get a little tipsy behind closed doors in the evening. I remember my mother's smile now, bless her. We were rich in love, and she gave her best.

We were in our school routine, and Damon and I started travelling to school ourselves, so Mum only took Alex. Mum was full of English pride. Even though she drank, she always kept up appearances and never let anyone look down on us. So to the outside world, we were like any average family. But on the inside, the cracks started appearing.

Alex had started primary school. I was in year five, and Damon was in year seven. We attended school strong-faced; home life wasn't too bad, but not perfect. Life was still great. We had friends, fun, and life ahead of us. After school, if we weren't playing computer, we'd be playing outside. Every kid from our street played football twenty metres from my house. All summer long, we played until dark. We were in our element, as Mum used to say.

We met the boxer, Nigel Benn, in our local chip shop. Luckily, we had a Sea Cadets club on our street, and Mum enrolled Damon and me. It was cheap, we attended twice a week, and their tuck shop had actual penny sweets. Those days when you could buy sweets for a penny, which was good value. We learnt how to salute correctly. Ships company halt. To the front, salute. Up, two, three, down.

Damon and I only attended for a few months, as we didn't fit in. There were about thirty people there, and Damon and I were the only non-white. We felt undesired, but it didn't faze us. Again, this goes back to feeling protected in my dual heritage. This was an exact moment that perspective helped me. My mum was white, and I loved her more than anyone. There was no feeling that any of those people felt that I couldn't relate to, if not improve upon.

The summers in Kennington were great. The latest craze was Tamagotchi, tiny mobile pets... Along with gooey little aliens that we genuinely believed grew. Damon and I still shared a bedroom, as Alex and Mum had the smaller rooms. We'd just got our own bedroom house phone, which was cool then. Nowadays, kids can use smartphones from a young age. My phone situation was like Jesus's sandal compared to your Nike Air Jordan's.

Damon was well into year seven, attending Salesian College Roman Catholic school in Battersea. This was great because he constantly learned exciting new things and shared that knowledge with me. I grew up faster because I learned everything from him. One summer's day, Mum played 'Sweet Like Chocolate' by Shanks and Bigfoot on repeat all day long; it's still one of my favourites. Music kept Mum going, and she loved to dance. She played old-school reggae songs like Minnie Riperton's 'Loving you.'

Mum always made sure we had something to eat. There were odd occasions when we'd run out of gas and electricity or have empty cupboards, but it wasn't regular. I'd look in the kitchen cupboard and find just out-of-date seasonings. Or only onion in the fridge. We had days when we struggled slightly, but I always stayed appreciative. I knew people were always in worse positions; some children didn't even have clean water. So, I was grateful for what I had. We weren't starving, and Mum always found a way to save the day. But her drinking soon got heavier, and she often got drunk.

Alex attended the after-school club, which finished at about five-thirty. This gave Damon or me enough time to get home and help Mum by picking him up. Alex waited for Mum to collect him from the after-school club a few times. But being intoxicated, she never made it. Once, I rushed to his school, and he was the only one waiting. It never bothered me; I liked the responsibility. But seeing the sad look on his face was a little disheartening.

Mum kept everything in line for a while but was literally an alcoholic before long. She needed a drink as soon as she awoke; otherwise, she'd shake and struggle. They weren't tremendous times, but we loved each other and tried our best to support her. Her drinking got worse, affecting Alex more as he was younger. Damon and I could considerably look after ourselves. Alex was big but only five, so he needed a strong parent figure.

This was when a significant change took place. Dad recognised that Alex's environment was unsuitable for a healthy upbringing, so he decided Alex must go and live with Grandma. We loved our brother dearly and didn't want him to leave, but he'd be in a more stable place. He was devastated; we were all he knew. As extremely close brothers, this rattled us all. When Dad tried to take him, Alex cried whilst hanging onto the staircase with all his might, screaming, 'I don't want to go. Nooooo.' Dad compassionately dragged him off to get him out the door. So, many tears were shed, and Alex was gone. Our brotherly threesome was over. It was just me, Damon, and Mum.

7

Just Us Three

The house was much quieter without Alex around and less fun too. Damon moved into Alex's old room, so we had our own bedrooms. Then Mum met Steve. He was Mum's new partner who lived around the corner. He seemed friendly, polite, and respectful. But we soon started spotting water bottles with foil and ash on the top, hidden in Mum's bedroom. We were unsure at first but eventually understood that these were crack pipes! Mum was now drinking and smoking crack.

I was almost eleven and not in a fantastic place. Mum still tried her best. Damon and I attended school brave-faced. We knew what Mum was doing wasn't right, but we were too young to fully understand. We were big enough to manage, though, so life continued gracefully. A few of our friend's parents also had drinking or drug issues, so we weren't the odd ones out. Two had it more challenging than us; their parents were on heroin. But we all stuck together and supported one another.

Because our parents had addictions, they were more lenient. So we could get away with more than your average kid. Within reason, of course, they weren't wattless. We'd play F-Zero X at our friend's house all night. We were good kids, though, full of innocence, and I was more into computer games than anything troublesome.

Mum was traditional and always bought us Christmas presents. But now, because she drank, we convinced her to give us money instead. We wanted

WCW versus NWO for our Nintendo 64, which was sixty pounds, an astonishing amount of money at the time. So, we went together to buy it from Elephant and Castle. We waited for the right time when no older boys were around, as we didn't want to get robbed. We bought it, Damon hid it in his trousers, and we ran half the way home!

My little bestie Bruno, the cat, and I were as tight as ever. Providing cat food was sometimes a predicament, but he was a survivor and still the hugest cat on the street. Damon met many new friends at secondary and started hanging out in Pimlico. It wasn't far, fifteen minutes' walk, just over Vauxhall bridge. He returned excited once after meeting a girl he liked. He said she looked like a white Jennifer Lopez! He never declared much because I was probably still the annoying little brother in his eyes. But I discovered her name was Michelle.

I didn't see as much of Damon those days, as he was always out with his friends. But it was all good, though; I had friends too. I had Jace and Jamal three minutes away, whose dad worked at our school. He was a Wing Chung black belt and taught us moves. We'd punch his stomach our hardest yet never hurt him. Besides copying Bruce Lee or the *Power Rangers*, it was my first taste of authentic kung fu. Dad had taught me some moves, but this was the real deal. I loved martial arts as a kid and dreamed of learning them one day. After school, I'd regularly visit Jace's house and watch *Countdown* with his mum and big sister Jade. I usually won the math ones.

Mum decided to rent Damon's room out for extra cash, so he moved back in with me. We weren't bothered. I think we preferred sharing; we got on well. A young Jamaican man named Diamond moved in for forty pounds a week. We snuck into his room once when he was out; he had a soap bar cut up next to a razor. We believed he was making up some fake crack. We thought, what idiot will buy this stuff? But he usually always came back smiling. He wasn't bad; probably just a product of his environment.

This was also the time I discovered *Zelda - The Ocarina of Time*. This game took over my life; I was addicted. It was the latest and greatest virtual reality game the world offered. An epic adventure, fighting evil to save a beautiful princess. It influenced and inspired me because I believed that I was just like

Link, the hero of *Zelda*.

Life's an adventure, with limitless possibilities, just like the game. So, I incorporated all the positive things I learned into my life. Whether that be acting courteously like Link or appreciating everything I had. Things weren't perfect, but I remained optimistic. I knew I was intelligent with great potential. I hoped it would all pay off one day if I stayed strong. The good guy always wins in the end, right? The movies, computer games, and my heart said so.

'An apple a day keeps the devil away,' Mum said. But sometimes, the berry does not taste so sweet in the thick of the action. One morning Mum came home with a big pair of sunglasses on, and we knew something was wrong. She took them off and revealed a huge black eye. She'd fought with our friend's mum. We weren't sure why, but Steve's name got mentioned. Too much alcohol was never a winning situation with Mum, and this was probably just that.

Her heart was good, but she was like *Jekyll and Hyde*. A wise, caring mother when sober and a monster when drunk. Like an event horizon with an alcohol limit, there was no turning back once crossed. Her heart was pure, but she would just get carried away. She'd fall over and hurt herself. Seeing Mum in pain was heartbreaking; it sometimes felt like we were the parents. She'd wake up the next day, face innocent like a Jaybird, without recollecting the previous night. Bless her; she'll always be my angel.

In September, I started year six, my last in primary school. Damon was a lot bigger than me by then. We both had crazy growth spurts, so I always played catch-up. Yo-yos had just become popular again. We all had one, usually from the one-pound shop, but Damon had a thirty-pound Viper. He had a paper round, getting thirteen pounds a week, which was a good amount for a twelve-year-old.

His friend, Sam, from the 'Pimlico crew', would call him on our house phone. I chatted with her for about half an hour; it was fun. Damon's female friends looked at me as his cute little brother and sometimes gave me sweet attention. I soon also saw what they don't teach in sex education. Damon was in big school, associating with elders. He brought home a videotape that enlightened me on what happens in the bedroom department. I was eleven, and until then, I knew about sex but never really knew how it was done. I sat, watching it. Suddenly, I got dizzy, and my body tingled. I didn't know what'd just happened, but it felt immense.

At the time, we were pretty used to our lifestyle. Even though Mum was an alcoholic crack smoker, she functioned ok. She ensured we didn't go without. 'By hook or by crook,' she said. So life revolved relatively smoothly, considering. We also acquired a PlayStation. Kelvin 'chipped' it for twenty-five pounds, enabling it to play counterfeit games. We got copied games for five pounds, a massive difference from the original cost of around forty.

We bought *Resident Evil*, *Tony Hawks*, *Metal Gear Solid*, and *Final Fantasy*, to name a few, which kept us going for hours. These games were usually the first in the series, so each was an exciting new adventure. He could also get CDs, and a talented rapper had just come out called Eminem. 'My Name Is' had recently exploded on the scene, which was unique. His album soon became our favourite.

The internet was about, but we didn't have a personal computer. So technological life for us consisted of music, Nickelodeon, and PlayStation. I had rinsed off all my Nintendo 64 games but sometimes played *Zelda* or *Super Mario*. I always got lost in *Zelda*, as that game held the integrity I based my life on. I applied the principles those games taught me in my own life. I believed that life was like them, but a lot greater and more advanced. I must be strong like the heroes of the games because life's journeys aren't simple.

Nothing good usually comes easily. Working hard for something is great; we appreciate it more when achieved. Life is like a computer game; you wouldn't want to turn it on, press one button, and complete the game with the princess saved. Where's the fun in that? Life's an adventure; getting there, with all the obstacles you overcome and how you grow from that, is where the treasure lies.

I wonder, if those games and movies positively influenced me, what effect does the demonic stuff the children see these days have on them? People dressed up like devils, lap-dancing for Satan; that's a kid's music video in 2021. Children are like sponges, soaking up all the information around them. The Devil uses these low blows because he doesn't know how to throw a clean punch. Clean versus dirty, two polar opposites. I chose the right one, not the left or the wrong. Freedom of expression is great but cursing and worshipping the Devil isn't favourable for children's eyes.

8

Starting Secondary School

T wo schoolfriends attended the cinema with me to see *The Mummy*, starring Brendan Frasier and Racheal Weisz. It was incredible, showcasing all the latest CGI. The summer holidays had returned, and I'd officially finished primary school. I'd soon join Damon in secondary.

Mum still drank and smoked, and we sometimes had a few undesirables in our house. She'd play music until the early hours, drinking downstairs while we tried to sleep on school nights. We awoke a few times to find our VCRs or computer consoles missing. Obviously stolen by a seedy associate of Mum's, who saw her as an easy target carrying her heart on her sleeve. Her tears of guilt, discovering we'd been robbed when sober in the morning, broke my heart and were more painful than losing any electronics. But Mum always made things right, eventually replacing them.

We were a household filled with love throughout the ups and downs. In 1999, Mum planned something spectacular, and no one spoiled the surprise this time. Our first trip abroad. A mystical adventure to Jamaica. The aeroplane ride was scary but worth it. We touched down, and the heat hit me like a slap. Boy, it was hot.

We had a lovely week in Ocho Rios and visited Kingston too. A man asked to buy Mum's trainers from her, it was funny, she had some exclusive Reebok Classics. We also purchased the latest rap CD, *Ruff Ryders-Ryde or Die Volume 1*, which became our new favourite. The late great DMX was on there, and Eve,

Drag-on, Styles P, and Jadakiss, to name a few. Swizz Beats was the leading producer. This seemed the most gangster music on the planet; these rappers were hard.

Cars in Jamaica drive extremely fast; oh, my, it was thrilling. A woman jumped to pass us our ball back while in the swimming pool, and her bra fell; that made us laugh. We also discovered that we had an all-inclusive holiday on the final day. So, we missed out on all the free food we were entitled to for the whole week. How on earth did Mum not know this? We enjoyed one day of all-inclusive food and then got packed to return to England.

Everything went smoothly; we had a pleasant flight and a safe landing. We were in the line going through checkout, and a lady with a baby was making lots of noise next to us. The security came over and started questioning Mum. They asked her how she acquired the money for a holiday to Jamaica as a single mother living off government benefits.

They took us to a table to search through our bags. As they opened a suitcase, I immediately noticed that all the clothes weren't ours. Instead, there was a bottle of wine and an adult-sized Manchester United shirt I'd never seen before. It was bright red, sticking right out. Shocked, I kept quiet. I was unsure what was happening but could sense something abnormal.

They took us to a different part of the airport and then took Mum away. It was just me and Damon left in the room with them. They asked us to remove our trainers and bend them to see if drugs were hidden inside. 'Would you like some chocolate or a magazine?' they humbly said. We weren't stupid and thought they were trying to sweeten us up.

They asked a few questions, and we told the truth; we didn't know anything. We knew the football shirt and everything else wasn't ours but kept quiet, acting unaware. Thank God, Mum never told me anything because I might've slipped up. Children are innocent and want to be the hero. Sometimes, the less they know about certain things, the better.

About three hours passed, and finally, Mum returned. She looked stressed and repeatedly said, 'I told you I've got nothing!' They'd taken Mum to the hospital because they suspected she was carrying drugs inside her; thank goodness she wasn't. We reunited, got our bags, and swiftly exited. Mum hailed the closest cab and got us out of there fast. She sighed hugely in the cab, saying, 'Thank God Almighty for that.' It drove us all the way home.

Mum always said we had angels watching over us that day. I later discovered that we did indeed carry drugs back to England in the suitcase's lining. Before the 9/11 terrorist attacks, airport security wasn't as stringent as it is now. So Mum got five thousand pounds and a free holiday. She later told me she did it because she wanted to get us decent school clothes and stuff. It was rather expensive for a single mother to provide for two children and two addictions. Especially considering we needed shoes, blazers, jackets, and bags, to say the least.

Mum also told me in later life that she had a small party and bought so much crack it covered her little glass table - to celebrate her success, of course. Considering that we got stopped, searched, and still got through. I sincerely believed in miracles from that day. God never wanted Mum taken away from us then, so His angels intervened. I've kept to that sort of principle my whole life. No matter the situation, keep faith in your heart, don't give in, and you'll persevere. That faith has never let me down, ever. Even in the harshest of odds, there's always some way through. David and Goliath, for instance, where a man was victorious over a giant. 'When there's a will, there's a way,' Mum would say. We got through that situation by the skin of our teeth, that's for sure.

Mum bought us all our new school gear and could afford some brand-named stuff. We were older and had started taking pride in our appearance. Kids mocked you if you attended school in non-designer clothes. When young, peer pressure is potent and influential. Damon led the way because I copied a lot from him. Mum bought us stylish Nike jackets, cool bags, and Ravel leather shoes. Damon got a new blazer, and I got his hand-me-down. Still, it wasn't in bad condition; it did the job, plus, it had all that good two years of energy and strength from him wearing it. We truly affect everything we have contact with; that's how psychics can pick up energy from anything we've touched.

The summer holidays drifted by, and once again, in September, we returned to school. But this time, I was starting secondary. This was an exciting new adventure. Unsure of how smart I really was, this was my chance to find out. The pitfall with Salesian College was that it was an all-boys school. School without girls...great. I took tests to decide what class I'd be in. There were five different classes. A, b, c, d, and e. I earned my way into the top class: seven e. This was tremendous. I *was* genuinely intelligent, and maybe I *could* still be a lawyer.

The older kids looked huge; some were bigger than the teachers. Luckily, I had Damon in year nine, so I also met his friends. Having an older brother to look out for me was hugely beneficial, helping my status. I met most of the popular boys in my year, and all of them, bar one, were in other classes. My class was full of 'boffins,' as we were called. Only me and two others were streetwise. One had an older brother in Damon's year. Just shows when we have an older sibling to learn from, we may grow up slightly faster. He became my best friend in my class. Our school was very multi-cultured, and probably 90% were of mixed heritage. But most of my friends were in the other classes.

There was this giant kid called, Alex, who was the biggest in our year. He was bolo. He was bigger than most of the year-eights and nines and soon took the role of the year bully. I didn't particularly like him because no honourable person likes a bully.

So I settled into secondary school life and turned twelve, and then Christmas came. Our first with just me, Damon, and Mum was quieter than usual, with fewer presents as we were older. We asked Mum for money to buy something we preferred instead. Mum, high on principles, always ensured we had a few presents to open. And a Christmas tree; we always had beautiful ones. It was smaller this year but manageable. Then came the millennium. We stayed home and watched fireworks from our window with Damon's friend, green-eyed Anthony. To me, it was nothing special, just another day.

The year 2000 was a significant milestone in human history. So much for the millennium bug. We were officially in a new century, the twenty-first. The big reset. That is what they thought might happen. What even was that? I didn't know, but the world didn't end, and no computer virus took down the internet. The big reset seems more current right now. We seem to be experiencing a genuine reset with the coronavirus pandemic. But in 2000, nothing changed; just another day.

Being bigger now, Damon managed to get me a paper-round job also. Eleven pounds a week paycheck. It's laughable now, thinking about that small wage because it took me forty minutes to complete and an hour on the weekends. The bag was huge, almost the same size as my back. I noticed what the shopkeeper was charging and the price of the newspapers. It seemed he was making hundreds of pounds while paying me eleven. But hey, it was money I didn't have. We both went to East Street Market and bought loads of sweets on payday.

Mobile phones designed with better technology had become vastly more popular. You could buy them in the shops for less than one hundred pounds, so almost everybody got one. I started hanging out with the rude boys in my year. Most were in the lower classes and not as intellectually dazzling, but we clicked. Maybe because I had an older brother or was intelligent and streetwise. I became friends with all the popular kids. Sometimes they joked, calling me a geek, but that never bothered me; I took it as a compliment. You can call me smart all day, no problem.

One mate was the tiniest guy in my year, making him an excellent thief. He could steal something from right underneath your nose without you even knowing. I think he came from a broken home because theft came naturally. I also became good friends with huge Alex. We'd hit East Street market, where they'd shoplift all sorts. They got hats and trainers, left from one stall and right from another, sometimes getting the wrong sizes. I was too timid to steal, unable to do it at first, but a point came where I had to contribute something. What other reality was there? Was I meant to go with them and just keep watching? No, it bothered them, so I had to participate. I cannot remember what it was, but I got something silly that didn't have much use. I got something, though, and that was what mattered.

I loved that Alex was big like Hercules. The London streets were tough, but my year seven friend was probably almost six feet tall already. He looked years older than he was, and I felt safe with him. We also went to phone shops, where they stole the phones on display before shops replaced them with dummies. Damon sometimes came home with stolen stuff as well; it seemed like we were all doing it. He had a new best friend, Anthony, from a few of his classes at school.

Later in 2000, Mum mentioned being offered a house swap to a much bigger house. Mum and Steve viewed it and said it was lovely. We had a little discussion and decided the bigger house seemed right. So, we left Kennington behind and moved to a four-bedroom house on Brixton Hill.

9

Brixton Hill

Elm Park was the name of our street, and it was directly opposite Brixton Prison. Steve drove us there and funnily carried Mum through the threshold. This house was massive; it had a basement, a study, four bedrooms, and two toilets. Damon and I had our own bedroom each, and we soon settled in. Mum rented the spare room to an older man from Trinidad and Tobago. He was lovely and enjoyed a beer sometimes, but he was a splendid lodger. His name was Mikey, and we called him Uncle.

We learned our new route: getting a bus down to Brixton Town centre and then another to Clapham Junction, usually walking the rest. Damon and I would travel to school most days and make our way home separately. Sometimes, there were problems on the bus because we had an unofficial beef with the other local school, Battersea Tech. They had plenty of 'bad boys,' and I heard gruesome stories of kids from our school getting robbed. So going to and from school required caution.

Once some boys were waiting in the alley next to our school; I recognized one from Battersea Tech. They let me walk by because I was too small, but one boy pulled out a mallet and hit a year ten in the face. He dropped to the floor; they searched his pockets and took his phone. My heart pounded, and as I safely made it through my school gates, I thanked God that I wasn't hurt. However, the year ten walked in holding his face with his mouth bleeding.

We were living in a new house, a new millennium, and a new start. We had officially settled into Brixton; life was sweet. I had recently bought a music creation game, *Music*, for my PlayStation, and I started making beats. Damon also tried smoking weed. I told him it was not for me; I'd never smoke it.

It soon came time for the halfway-through-the-year exams. I got the highest grade in mathematics in my class, which was top, so I got the highest result in my year. Number one out of around 140 boys. Not bad, hey? This result gave me more drive for life because it proved that I was a protege. My future was looking bright.

Soon, my intrigue towards the weed Damon smoked overpowered me. My first time was just us two; I took a few puffs. Oh my goodness, I felt like I was sinking into the bed. Things that weren't that funny suddenly made me laugh like crazy. That first time felt exhilarating. Before long, I smoked some more, and we both started enjoying it. But we only smoked it occasionally as we never had money to buy it.

Upon moving to Brixton, we had quit our paper rounds as we didn't have enough time to get to Kennington early before school. So, we lost eleven and thirteen pounds a week combined. Mum offered us a lifeline. We could share a room, rent the spare one and keep the money. It would put some cash in our pockets. Damon and I were soldiers; we could share again, no problem. It'd be fun. Of course, we agreed, as we got on well, the rooms in our new house were massive, and we wanted the money.

Mum rented the room for sixty pounds a week to a Trinidadian lady called Mavis. But she gave us the rent from Uncle Mikey, who paid forty. So Mum increased her weekly incomings by one hundred pounds by renting out rooms. Damon and I got twenty pounds each, every Friday, and you can imagine what we mostly spent that on. Yes, every Friday was a miniature party at ours. We were officially stoners.

We sometimes took days off school if we wanted, as Mum's situation gave her limited authority over us. However, she was still as strict as possible and upheld all her responsibilities. Bruno was in his prime then, and he ruled the street again. He'd walk on the pavement and not even move when a human walked past. But he caught fleas, which weren't pleasant.

We soon got ourselves mobile phones. Damon was older and always ahead of me, so he got one first. He got a Nokia 5110, the first model with an interchangeable front cover - all the rage. He gave it to me upon acquiring a better Nokia 3210. We could always keep in touch, but phone calls were costly, like thirty pence a minute, so a ten-pound credit didn't last long. It could finish in one half-an-hour phone call.

Damon's best friend Anthony regularly visited. We played computer games, listened to music, and rapped to my beats. It was our first Brixton summer; I was twelve. Brixton was lively, so we soon started meeting people. Damon, Anthony, and I would sit in the front room. Pretty girls would walk past our window all day. We'd jump up to the curtains, barging each other to get a look-in. If they noticed, they'd usually smile, and we sometimes ran outside to speak to them, but we were still young and shy.

We also took up rollerblading and went on adventures all over London. Locally we had Stockwell Ramps, only fifteen minutes' walk away, the best open skate park in south London. We'd skate up and down, do stunts, and replicate the older, more advanced skaters, getting a good few bumps and bruises along the way. Damon tried a backflip once and failed terribly. I initially laughed, but it wasn't funny because he'd hit his head and hurt himself. We'd also hit Kennington and Battersea Park, having tremendous times. We'd skate over anything, copying the moves we learned in games like *Tony Hawks*, trying our best to grind.

Damon also brought home intriguing things, like the latest music he discovered. There was a new song, 'Here With Me,' by Dido, who also featured on Eminem's song, 'Stan.' I loved it and listened to her *No Angel* album every day. I was unsure why because I was more into hip-hop and garage, but this album took me.

That summer, a blonde girl walked past us outside our house, and Damon asked her for a cigarette. We pulled the cigarette manoeuvre to spark conversations; sometimes, it worked. Her name was Sarah. I can't remember the ins and outs, but she returned with an older boy named Cold a few hours later. He was seventeen, had a huge afro, and showed us a big wooden kitchen knife inside his jacket pocket. He asked if we were causing Sarah any trouble. We assured him we weren't; I think she fancied Damon because we all became friends by the end of the conversation. I was twelve and knew a Brixton boy who carried a knife!

Mum still drank and smoked and had a new boyfriend named Desmond, who everyone called Dez. He had schizophrenia and was a little crazy, but his heart was clean. As an alcoholic, he reinforced Mum's drinking; she now drank twenty-four-seven. Yet, despite the circumstances, she never failed to love us.

They missioned to East Street market, got drunk, and listened to CD players wearing giant headphones. It was a little embarrassing being seen with them, but I loved Mum dearly and had faith in her. Once, I was with them on the top deck of a bus. Dez needed the toilet, so he peed right there next to himself! That was the ugly reality of alcoholism.

Over time, we became very close with our lodgers and considered them family. Aunty Mavis had a brother called Bryson, a Trinidadian yardie gangster. Scarface was his nickname, as he had a large scar across his cheek. He owned a few stalls at the start of East Street Market from which he sold American-style apparel. I'm sure his hands were in many pies, as he always had a pocket full of cash. Like me, he was a ladies' man, and I'll mention no more. I'll just say I heard a few funny noises coming from Uncle Mikey's room when Bryson borrowed it. He sometimes gave me work helping on his hat stall, earning me twenty pounds daily. This was good money considering my previous employer paid me eleven pounds weekly. He also took me to the circus with him and a lady. He used me as cute innocent bait to sweeten her up and mentioned me helping him get lucky.

Soon Damon and Sarah became an item, and she only lived five minutes away. Her friend Michelle was Nigerian and Vietnamese; man, she was stunning. She was slightly above my league, but Anthony tried his luck before discovering she had a boyfriend. Sarah's older brother James was seventeen and hench, a real G. He looked out for us. He nicked the odd C90 pizza bike and joyrode us around locally. Our house got a little hectic sometimes, as we had two lodgers, and Mum and Dez were drinkers. But being young, life was fun.

I soon saw *The Matrix*. This movie was spectacular and perfectly fitted into my existence. I believed I could be like Neo in real life. Maybe I could be the one to save the world. Why not? To our knowledge, we're living in the first world that ever existed, so anything is possible, right? Anyone had the potential to be the one, and whoever fits the mould best could maybe fulfil that role. It reinforced my belief in how extraordinary life could really be.

I started year eight and got the highest result on the math tests again! Whoopie doo. I was literally the smartest kid in my year because the teachers said mathematics is the basis of understanding. It's a universal language and the foundation of all knowledge. Because life at home was unstable, my school attendance faltered. I never really had to go in if I didn't want to. Dad wasn't around to spank us, and Mum got angry if we disobeyed her; but because we were bigger, there was only so much she could physically do. She wanted the best for us and tried her utmost to be responsible. Still, because of addiction, her authority was limited. I wanted to attend because I knew skipping school and missing vital information wasn't beneficial.

I sometimes spotted a few members of So Solid Crew while walking to school as they grew up in Battersea. A new cartoon grabbed my attention: *Dragon Ball Z*. Everyone talked about it at school. Every day I rushed home to watch it at 5pm. It was funny because it left cliffhangers daily to ensure you returned. Sometimes it took almost a week for one fireball to be completed; it was the Cell and Frieza saga. It was cool. We stuck to our school, television, smoking weed, and rollerblading routine.

I was great at making beats, and people loved my lyrics. I practised at home and battle rapped in school. I was a talented wordsmith and was admired as a top emcee. These were the days of underground garage music, and MC Wiley was a key pioneer. His *Eskimo* songs were a favourite beat to rap to.

I then saw *Titanic*. I smoked a spliff before watching to get the motions going. Oh, my goodness, I fell in love with this movie; it's still my favourite today. It's funny; I portrayed myself as a streetwise, ghetto youth from Brixton. But deep down, I was just a romantic. For months, I watched *Romeo and Juliet* every night to put myself to sleep. There's an insight into not judging a person or book by appearance. You never know what emotions are indeed hiding beneath the skin or pages.

I soon turned thirteen. I was accustomed to secondary. I made more friends, one being Damon's bestie Anthony's younger cousin, Tony, who came from America. I also met a quiet boy named Richard, who we called Mousy; he quickly became my best friend. I no longer really hung with huge Alex. He flaunted his power and tried bullying Mousy, beating him up a little. He did the same with Tony. When Anthony found out, he wanted to give him a taste of his own medicine, so he caught him after school. It wasn't easy because Alex was humungous. Still, Anthony was strong, and Alex wisely took his defeat because of Anthony's age and status advantage, so he got beaten up a little. He acted differently after this, becoming slightly humbler. It just shows no matter how big and bad you are, there's always someone bigger and stronger.

Damon started to spend more time with his girlfriend, Sarah. One day, when I was walking down behind Tulse Hill estate, I saw her. I called out, but surprisingly, it wasn't Sarah. Instead, it was a cute girl named Caren, and I got her number. We texted back and forth the next day, and I soon asked her out; she said yes. So, I had my own beautiful girlfriend. We walked around Brockwell Park together for hours, talking about everything underneath the sun. She was one year younger than me and always looked pretty, with perfume so sweet that the smell became a significant memory. She was my first girlfriend, which was an all-new, exciting experience.

10

Teenage Years

Homelife became even more dysfunctional because Mum was associating with other drinkers and smokers locally. Brixton Hill was notorious for drugs and prostitution. I believe our house played a significant role in escalating that fact. Ours was like a stop-off point for the local prostitutes to smoke after grafting their money from punters. It was still a family home; they must've liked the normality compared to other places. They probably felt safe; we had two solid Caribbean lodgers who protected the house with their presence alone. They always had family over, so loud Trinidadian accents regularly came from their rooms, bringing a lovely, homely aura to an otherwise chaotic household.

Their Rastaman friend, Dexter, also known as Janx, smoked weed religiously and sometimes associated with us. He sold weed and had loads of money and gold. Once, he fell asleep in our front room, and Mum stole £230 out of his pocket. I witnessed it all. She was there for twenty minutes sneaking her two fingers into his jean pocket, pulling out more and more money. I advised her not to do it; it was unwise. 'Mum, leave him some money.'

'No, I'm taking it all.' When Janx awoke, Mum was gone, and he went berserk, bursting into a rage, screaming the house down, 'Me want my bomboclat money.' He wouldn't leave until he got his supposed three hundred pounds back.

Mum returned home the next day, acting innocent like she had no idea. 'I don't know who took your money. Janx; it must've been someone who was here.' She blamed it on a random smoker, and I definitely wasn't gonna grass her up. He probably suspected Mum but settled by saying, 'How you let people rob me while me asleep. You never watch mi back?' He stayed for three days until somehow, Mum managed to get him three hundred pounds. He left instantly, cussing all the way out the door.

Another time, he demanded sex from a prostitute, screaming, 'Gimme the pum-pum! Me want the pum-pum!' He then hit her face with a beer can, splitting her cheek wide open. Bless her; she didn't deserve it at all. These are just some of the many episodes in our manic household.

My girlfriend, Caren, would visit me at home with her cousin. But I was embarrassed to invite her inside because it wasn't exquisite. We hadn't carpeted our whole house, and Bruno had fleas on top of the other issues. So, we'd hang out outside my house for hours, flirting away. We did this for a few months until, one day, I invited her in. She'd never seen *The Matrix*, so we watched it together on my bed. She said nothing bad about my home but asked, 'Why have you got no carpet in your bedroom?'

'We're getting it carpeted soon,' I replied. The next day she texted me, saying she was breaking up. She never stated why but just said it was over. And that was the end of that relationship. I knew it wasn't me but my home that had put her off. I was upset because she was sweet, but we hadn't developed deep feelings so young, so I moved on.

I found the book *The Lion, the Witch, and the Wardrobe* in my house. Oh, my goodness, it was fantastic; I was addicted. I hid in Mum's room for privacy, as she was always out, sometimes for days. I read the entire book in under forty-eight hours! It was so encapsulating that I couldn't put it down. The first time I'd been taken into another world through words alone. It stimulated my imagination so much upon completion that I soon found and read *The Magicians Nephew*, the series' first book.

Mousy and Anthony lived in Kennington, so we spent most of our time between there and Brixton Hill. I felt more comfortable in Kennington because we had many friends from living there. Brixton was notoriously one of the roughest places in London. Before social media, graffiti was rife and a fundamental way to increase your notoriety. Certain tags, as they were called, were everywhere locally: Cosa, Dopes, and Ninja, to name a few. I'd used some myself, like Plasma and Plague, but I settled on Duppy. I got this from a brief period in primary school when we learned about the Caribbean. Duppy, the Jamaican word for ghost, seemed perfect. We left our tags on every bus and any new areas we went to show we'd been there. A bit like a cat peeing to mark its territory in one way. Life at this young age was always a new adventure.

Mum played music loud in the summertime. She loved cooking and said she learned from my grandmother, who taught her how to cook delicious Jamaican food. We soon met someone who became known to us as Uncle Denny. He grew up with our uncles and biological father, who I'd not mentioned thus far. That's because our birth parents split when we were incredibly young. Our father, Everton Grossett, didn't play a significant role in our early childhood. He was a hard-working, kind gentleman. But because of their separation, it worked out that way.

He and Aunty Charmaine took us to McDonald's when I was five. We drove, and I always got car sick. Upon entering, the food smell triggered me. Charmaine ran for a cup, which I threw up in. Unfortunately, it wasn't big enough, and the sick burst everywhere; we left without any McDonald's.

He posted the odd fifty-pound note through our door before Christmas when we were young. My biological father is no longer here; he is with Mum in Heaven. He passed away from a heart attack four months after being in the Croydon Tram crash of 2016. It played a crucial role in his death because it had a significant adverse effect on him. He later passed away at only fifty-five years old, the same age my mother passed. May he forever rest in peace.

2001 was the year a pioneering music group, So Solid Crew released their debut number-one hit single, '21 Seconds.' When I first saw the video, I was ecstatic, as nothing had really been done like this before. It contained a gang of emcees, and their video used cool special effects. This song brought a whole new sound and era to mainstream music. It was a crucial moment in the foundation of modern music that dominates today.

Uncle Denny gave us a gigantic sixteen-inch speaker the size of a small fridge, on which we blared music at full volume all day and night. You could hear it from the top of our street, well over 100 metres away! It never phased me then, but in hindsight, I feel sorry for our neighbours because we played music full whack, even at 3:00am. We had forty-seven noise complaints.

The Marshall Mathers LP by Eminem was like my unofficial tutor growing up, and 'Stan' was my favourite song. I idolized rappers and wanted to be just like them. So, I feel sorry for today's youth because current drill music usually glamourises nothing but violence, and music highly influenced my thoughts and actions. From experience, youngsters want to fit in and impress older youth; so, what chance do kids stand these days in the current gun, knife, and gang culture? I'd hate to grow up in London today. It's a warzone, and I'm pretty sure I would've been caught in the mix.

Mum loved her Bashment music and got all the latest CDs from the market, like Sizzla, Vybes Cartel, and Elephant Man. She loved ragga, and we started liking it too. Damon turned fifteen in the summer and was a young man. We still shared a bedroom, so I pretended I was asleep when he and Sarah had sex. That wasn't fun but rather intriguing.

One day Mum was a little drunk and played around, whipping us with a wet towel. She accidentally caught Damon in the eye. He ragefully fly-kicked Mum with all his might. She flew across the room and smashed her head on the wall, bursting into tears. I was so disappointed with him; it broke my heart.

My school attendance worsened, and I came second in math on end-of-year tests. I smoked skunk weed almost daily and bunked off school regularly, so it wasn't long before my number one rank was lost. Coming second was good, but my dream of becoming a lawyer was out the window. I then wanted to make it in the music industry. I'd created over one hundred beats and was good at it. So I'd bunk off school and stay home with a local friend called Credit. We'd smoke weed and rap to the beats I made all day, recording them onto cassettes.

Damon introduced me to all the latest rap CDs. I liked Nas and Styles P. Nas was my favourite because he was an eloquent wordsmith with a hard-hitting style. We idolized these rappers, listening to their music religiously. I started reading the Bible quite a bit, as I'd always believed in God. I'd even read it high, which I don't recommend. I sometimes misinterpreted the information in this state, thinking there were hidden meanings. When we're under the influence of substances, our perception is altered, and it's not a good state to be reading a holy book.

We soon bought a Sega Dreamcast, which had better graphics than our previous consoles, which kept us busy. I also met a boy who lived a few doors down the road named Jason. He looked up to me, and we became good friends.

That summer, Damon, Mum, and my relationship became volatile. We argued, usually over silly things. Finally, Mum decided she couldn't handle our unruliness at that rebellious teenage stage, where you're no longer a child yet far from an adult. So, she contacted our father, Everton, 'Come and take your children; I can't handle them anymore.' So, we packed a few things and went to live with him.

He lived near Tooting Bec, so this was an all-new experience. It felt like we were meeting him for the first time. His girlfriend, Rita, who he'd been with since leaving Mum, was a retired chef whose cooking was incredible. My father was a security guard and part-time DJ, playing music in a pub every weekend. So we'd help them set up and have a good old time. Afros had recently re-spawned as cool, so I grew a huge one, looking like Toad from *Super Mario*.

That year, I entered year nine and Damon started year eleven. I got his old blazer again as his colour changed from burgundy to black. Dad's was fun, and we cut down on smoking weed as he had standard parent rules. We soon met two of Rita's nephews. Leon, our age, and Lil Dillan, five; we called them cousins. They lived next door to Keisha Buchanan from Sugababes. I turned fourteen, and my school attendance improved; we went every day. Christmas soon came, and we entered 2002.

We missed Mum and had slight problems with Dad. We preferred being at Mum's, maybe because Dad was stricter. Early that year, we returned home to Brixton after roughly six months. Mum was ecstatic; she'd missed us dearly. However, our lodgers said things had only worsened. 'This house is like a crack house; I'm moving out soon.' We didn't want this because they kept the house safe.

11

A Young Man

One day, Celeste came around to see us; Damon, more so than me. She was Damon's age, but he wasn't home. I thought this could be my time tonight. I remember the date; the 2nd of the 2nd 2002, a lucky day for me. At fourteen years and three months, I lost my virginity. It was a race to achieve this because the older two of our four-person crew had already done the deed. I didn't want to be last; luckily, I beat Mousy to it. I didn't know what I was doing, but it went OK. The boys cheered when I told them; it was like winning the lotto. Mousy could not yet relate.

It wasn't long before Aunty Mavis found somewhere else and was gone just like that. Her smile highlighted her relief in leaving all the drama behind. Mum soon got a new lodger, a man named Newton, an ex-semi-professional boxer with boxing equipment who loved teaching us. Life was still great; being young, we always found a way to have fun.

Once, Sarah's friend, Michelle's boyfriend, a boy called Itchy from Poinders in Clapham, argued with Damon on the phone. It was over something silly, but ego influences one's life at that young age, so they both gave it the large. They went back and forth, cursing each other.

This later affected us because Damon, Anthony, Sarah, Michelle and I walked through Poinders a few weeks later as Itchy walked by. Michelle said, 'Oh no, there's Itchy.' He was with his nineteen-year-old cousin Tank and others. They immediately recognized us and started attacking Damon.

Mid-brawl, Damon was knocked into the road, narrowly missing a honking car. One punched me, so I ran. I thought Damon and Anthony took off the other way. I jogged home and soon met up with the others, and we went and got Sarah's older brother, James.

He was seventeen and had a car but no license. He put a large kitchen knife up each sleeve, and we drove straight back to Poinders. He had our back for sure. James was militant, and upon arriving, we searched but never found them, so we returned home. I was glad we didn't catch them because although I wanted revenge, I knew things would've only worsened if we'd seen them. That wasn't a great night; poor Damon got the worst of it. Reputation was crucial at that age and is something the youth kill for nowadays.

Mousy soon lost his virginity and became quite a ladies' man. Yes, he soon knew more pretty girls than all of us; once again, those who were last shall be first. He introduced me to a girl from Kennington named Zara, who became my girlfriend. These were the days of the Nokia 3310, and we all had one.

I started a little business selling snacks in school. I bought my stock from the market and then sold them twice the price I paid, making a few extra pounds profit every day. 'Crisps, drinks, muffins,' I'd regularly holler during breaks. I soon became fully dedicated to street life; growing up surrounded by gang culture, everybody wanted good street cred. I also took pride in getting as high as possible - smoking weed and sometimes sniffing lighter gas. The gas was intense and extremely dangerous; inhaling it could kill.

Dad gave Damon a laptop to help him with his schoolwork, but Damon never really used it. So he contacted Uncle Terry, with whom I made a song when I was seven. He loaded our laptop with all the latest music creation software, such as 'Fruity Loops,' 'Cubase,' and 'Logic Pro.' This was incredible; it upgraded my beats from the PlayStation level to something more official. But, of course, I never knew how to use any software, so through trial and error, I figured it out. I eventually settled on using 'Fruity Loops,' which seemed the simplest to configure.

We soon met our lodger Uncle Newton's two sons, Aaron, seventeen, and Newray, eighteen. They lived in Pollards Hill, and I loved having older companions; excellent protection. The summer holidays returned, and this was Damon's last in secondary school. The summer was eventful as we were more young men than boys.

I also met another girl named Trula, with whom I had a few sexual experiences. Once, she and Zara were both in my house unknowingly together. I preferred Zara, and even though we'd never slept together, she was prettier and got more attention. So I slipped between rooms, keeping Trula upstairs and Zara down, asking Mousy and Damon to keep Trula busy.

Uncle Mikey soon followed in Aunty Mavis's footsteps finding somewhere else to live. Mum got another lodger, a kind African student who looked like the rapper Akon. At forty pounds a week, he didn't complain much about the noisy, half-hostile environment. Mum was officially one of the most streetwise women on Brixton Hill and had many notorious friends. She knew most smokers, drinkers, and the shady people that Brixton offered. Even though our house had regular crack smokers visiting, Mum still cooked and treated us well.

Mum's American friend, Maurice, left Damon thirty ten-pound crack rocks to sell. 'I'll come back for the money tomorrow.' He never returned, so Damon smoked some in a spliff. I took two puffs, getting me high and tingling my body. I was fourteen and had tried crack cocaine. Then, Damon met Reagan, a yardie drug dealer with a crack house in Tulse Hill Estate. He offered him a job there selling drugs.

After two days, Damon returned home briefly, telling me about the dramas he had witnessed. One funny story was how someone got hit with a shovel over a twenty-pound rock. He'd barely slept two hours but had to return immediately. After a week, he returned frustrated, tired, and throttled, 'I got robbed.'

A Yardie stuck a gun in his face, saying, 'Where is the food? You wanna die?' Damon gave him everything - a wise decision. Reagan soon found out, and realizing Damon was only sixteen, he seemed ashamed. He thought he was older; otherwise wouldn't have put him there. We heard that Reagan had discovered who'd robbed his stash within twenty-four hours and got his drugs back, selling them with someone else in the same flat the next day. Just shows the world can be a small place sometimes, so be careful what you do on your doorstep.

Mum had a new partner, a twenty-nine-year-old Jamaican man named Andrew, and Mum loved him a lot quickly. The Notting Hill carnival soon came around, so we got our boys together and met with a massive group of older youths from Kennington. This was great, there were over thirty of us altogether, and we took up the entire top deck on the bus.

The rapper Tower T, who made the song 'You Can't Come to the Roadside' with the Roadside Geez, was with us. He was Anthony's mate, and this was my first carnival. It was fun but a little dangerous, as gangs from all over London attended. I felt safe, though, as we had enough backup.

The carnival is held in west London, and my school friend, probably the then toughest guy in my year, lived in Shepherd's Bush. I spotted him in a vast gang of about seventy at Rampage, the roughest part. He stood with a bandana over his mouth, staring intimidatingly at everyone. His audacity impressed me, as he was only fourteen but wasn't fazed by anyone. My Uncle Gammospeng was also DJing on one of the carts.

That summer was eventful, and in September, I entered year ten. Damon started college at St. Frances Xavier, where Tiny Temper attended. I hung around more with Aaron, going to house parties and raves. At fifteen, my school attendance really declined. In one term, it was 18%! Meaning I averaged under one day a week. I was more interested in making music. I also might've been experiencing a slight undercover depression. I was at that confusing age between childhood and adulthood, where you don't know yourself.

I acquired some Hitachi HSJ2 speakers and a keyboard from Aunty Lorraine, so I converted our home study into a mini studio. I also bought some cheap headphones and a microphone from Argos, so I had everything I needed. This became my all, and I spent hours making music; it was my dream. We all loved emceeing, especially Anthony and me, so we recorded a few songs and burnt them onto CDs. One was great; I'm sure it would've done well if I'd released it. It was 2002, and there was rarely any music similar to what we created; we were ahead of our time. In hindsight, I could've made it if I'd released my music correctly.

Because of our lifestyle, we didn't take care of Bruno wholeheartedly. Mum bought a flea collar, but the fleas returned, and he had a gammy eye infection. Then, one day, a neighbour knocked on our door, holding a cardboard box. Mum burst into tears. 'Dan, don't look.' Bruno's skull was split open, with his eye hanging out of his head. He'd been hit by a car, a sight I'll never forget. I felt guilty because I noticed that Bruno had lost his zeal for life. After all, we'd slacked with his maintenance. And just like that, my oldest friend was gone. We had a concrete garden with nowhere to bury him, so, against Mum's advice, we just binned the box in a neighbour's bin later that night.

Mum surprisingly had also become pregnant, so we'd soon have another sibling. She reduced but continued to drink and smoke. She preached to everyone how lovely we, her sons, were. One night Mum returned home with two girls aged sixteen and seventeen. They'd met her in Brixton. She had told them we were handsome and they should meet us. Mum was drunk, so they ensured she got home safely and wanted to meet us. I was too young, but Damon kissed the sixteen-year-old. Mum was rowdy; she even chatted up girls for us.

It soon turned 2003, the days when camera phones took off. So, many people were doing 'happy slapping.' You recorded someone as you slapped them, something I disapproved of and never participated in. But they were funny to watch sometimes, as savage as they were.

I attended more house parties and decided to throw one myself. I invited a few people, planning a gathering of maybe forty; we had only designated our front room. But the word spread like wildfire, and hundreds turned up, many we never knew. Most of the local Tulse Hill Estate gang arrived. About ten random guys even knocked on the door; one said, 'Some girls on the bus mentioned a party, so we thought we'd check it out.' But my house was already packed. One came inside and realized there was no space to move, so he left, saying, 'We gotta party somewhere else.' We were crammed in like sardines in a tin.

Mum was heavily pregnant, but everyone showed respect, and she mostly stayed upstairs. Someone noticed we were playing music from an mp3 player and called their DJ friend, who brought his decks and DJs all night. A little table was broken, and some mess was made, but it was a legendary house party.

I'd regularly link Aaron and his boys from Pollards Hill, like Ohzie and Septer. We'd go to Epsom to rob people's phones. I'm not proud, but many from my environment did it. I spotted a guy with the latest phone, the Nokia 8310. It was tiny, the craze everybody wanted. He was amid a phone call; I snatched it and sprinted off.

After a robbery, we'd jump straight on a train because the police would arrive quickly and immediately attend the train station as they knew we weren't local residents. Sometimes, we'd hide in the park if the train weren't there swiftly and wait for the police to leave. But it was tricky because the final train was just after eleven o'clock. There weren't any more until the following day; the police knew this. Once, we missed it and were stranded until the morning train, staying in the park all night.

In Reigate, we committed a robbery, and the police stopped our train from leaving. Ohzie had robbed a phone, and spotting the police, he quickly threw it under a train seat. They questioned and searched us but found nothing. Almost leaving, one officer looked around the carriage for evidence. He found the phone, and we all got arrested. 'Oi Dupz, say no comment,' Aaron reminded me. We got taken to Reigate police station and interviewed; I followed Aaron's advice.

They confiscated our clothes and trainers to process DNA evidence, giving us flimsy paper bodysuits and sponge shoes. We got bailed the next day, and lucky me, I was under sixteen, therefore a minor, so the police drove me home The others made their own way home with just train tickets. They said it was embarrassing walking through Victoria Train Station in the paper suits with everybody staring. Street robberies were something all too familiar growing up in my era.

12

Street Life

I was robbed on the way to school once. The rare time I had ten pounds in my pocket, a boy approached me, said something, and then punched me. He took my money just as two other boys followed. I knew one of them from Tulse Hill Estate called, Ceas. He acted innocent. 'Ceas, that guy just took my ten pounds.'

'Call me later; I'll try and get it back for you,' he said. I had his number as I bought weed from him sometimes, so I rang him after school. I realized my money was gone; he probably enjoyed the spoils with his accomplices. Live by the sword, die by the sword, as they say.

A few local boys were outside our house talking to us one day. I went inside, and Damon soon followed, looking shocked. 'Oh my God. Ninja's in a car with a sawn-off shotgun and a big grin.' I went out to look and walked past, but I didn't want to look stupid by staring as I never knew Ninja personally. He'd put it away, or I just walked past too quickly, but I knew Damon wasn't lying.

My life revolved around acquiring weed and making music. On the 26th of March 2003, I bunked off school and was desperate for weed, so I went out to try and make some money. I was on Streatham High Road when I spotted a suited businessman using the latest phone. The Beckham phones, we called them, as David Beckham was the leading advertiser on TV. They were costly, around five hundred pounds, and were cutting-edge technology with a big colour screen and camera.

I walked up to him mid-phone call, snatched it, and ran. 'Hey,' he shouted and gave chase. He looked over forty, so I thought he wouldn't pursue me; I was wrong. I ran my fastest, but he was on my tail every time I looked back. How was this possible? He must've gone to the gym. After a few minutes, I was breathless, and as he was still there a few meters behind me, I threw his phone back. That didn't go to plan.

I jogged back up to the main road and hopped onto a bus. I heard sirens getting close, and just as the bus pulled off, a police car pulled in front and stopped it. They came on and arrested me; as they did, a few passengers defended me, saying, 'Leave him alone; what has he done wrong? He's just a kid.' If they only knew. They took me to Streatham Police Station, only a few minutes away; no wonder they got to me rapidly. I discovered the man called the police immediately after I threw his phone back.

I never knew how the judicial system worked, so I was honest during the interview. Luckily, because I hadn't touched the guy or said anything, I got charged with theft from a person instead of robbery, which significantly differentiated the punishment's severity. Mum collected me because I was a minor. I got a criminal record and a six-month youth offending program as my sentence. It was easy; I attended fortnightly appointments to discuss a positive way forward, which I completed without any problems.

On the 27th of May 2003, at thirty-eight years old, Mum gave birth to my little brother, Tyreese. This was great. After a brief period in the hospital, she brought him home. Mum reduced her drinking and smoking; he wasn't mistreated or neglected. Once or twice, Mum, slightly drunk, put him in my arms, 'Dan, look after your little brother.' I didn't mind; it was fun having a baby brother exploring his new emotions.

We started hanging around Pimlico a lot more. Michelle, the girl Damon fancied when young, became his girlfriend. She was lovely, very kind, and didn't smoke or take drugs. She positively influenced Damon, and his mentality changed from street to normality. Michelle's mum, Debbie, older brother Michael, and sister Tina were all lovely. They were devout Christians, which Damon and I also became. We attended church with them on Sundays, which was fun, being around positive people.

I also met a Pimlico girl, Tasia, who soon became my girlfriend. We didn't sleep together, but it was exciting all the while. One day walking with her, a boy threw a plastic bottle at us, just missing me. I looked back and gave him a sour look. 'Is there a problem?' he rudely said.

'No, of course not.' I carried on walking. But there was a problem indeed. Who was he to throw a bottle at me? I'm from Brixton, and this guy from 'posh' Pimlico thinks he can embarrass me in front of my girl. That afternoon, I phoned Aaron, 'There's a guy we need to teach a lesson.'

'No problem, I'll link you soon, Dupz.' A few hours later, I met with Aaron, Septer, and Ohzie. We met Tasia, and I told her we'd get that boy back for what he'd done. She said, 'Oh no, these are big men. This will cause me problems.' I was more interested in ego and pride, so we waited outside his school.

Around 3:30pm, I spotted him. 'Remember me,' I said, then punched him twice. My boy's had my back, as he also had his school friend's backup. He was much bigger than me, and after a few punches, a crowd gathered, so we retreated. We quickly vacated, returning over the bridge to Vauxhall, and then jumped on the first bus towards Brixton. His strength surprised me; he ate my punches and continued forward. Still, we celebrated our victory, reliving the craziness of what happened.

In hindsight, I realized how unnecessary my actions were that day. The problems it ultimately caused me far outweighed the benefits. I was young, egotistical, and lacking wisdom, as many youngsters seem to be. He went to Tasia's school, which caused her problems; she even mentioned leaving. We broke up shortly after.

The karmic fear I experienced was essentially the trauma creator that plagued my thoughts negatively long after the incident. I avoided Pimlico to avert seeing him and looked over my shoulder when near there for years; I even avoided him in dreams. I bumped into him once. Outnumbered, I sprinted straight to Michelle's. Luckily, it was summer, so their door was open; I ran straight in. Just making it, I slammed the door behind me. Debbie ran towards me, shocked. 'Someone's chasing me who's gonna beat me up. I'm sorry. Please don't open that door,' I breathlessly whimpered.

We looked out the window to see him walking off while cussing, 'Pussy hole.' Every action has a reaction, and the karma you create will return to you eventually. Over those next few years, I definitely learned that.

In 2003, I finished year ten. Damon had a part-time job, so he bought a Black Typhoon 125 moped for three hundred pounds from Newray's friend, Flint. We raced it around locally, having great fun. I'd never ridden one before, so I could only get on the back while Aaron rode. After a few days, Flint decided he wanted more and demanded that Damon pay another one hundred pounds.

Aaron, our moped expert, didn't think it was worth it, so Damon told Flint he wasn't paying. He threatened Damon, who didn't seem that bothered. Aaron and Newray said Flint was nothing to worry about. A few days later, on a hot day during the summer holidays, Flint stated that he knew where we lived and was coming to collect his money. Damon spoke with Aaron and Newray and decided he still wasn't paying. So, we got our closest friends around, about eight of us. We wondered if this would be enough, so I suggested checking if the local boys could help us.

Damon, Mousy, and I walked into Tulse Hill Estate to find the man-dem. We knew they were tough and streetwise and spotted a few at the basketball court. 'Some boys from Pollards Hill are tryna bring beef to the ends. We need some backup.'

'Are you mad, fam? No youths can come around here and try bad up the manor. They'll get brock up.' They were happy and willing to defend us and their area. They said they'd be around near ours shortly. This was a huge morale boost, and about thirty turned up near ours. We were ready; our opponents wouldn't stand a chance.

Posted about forty meters from my house near the shop, we waited for Flint's arrival. The sun blazed away, and we waited. An hour passed, and they were not there. Then two. Where were they? We'd managed to get the whole gang on top of the eight of us, and they were no-shows. Some left and said to phone if they arrived. Another hour passed, the gang returned, and the opposition still hadn't shown up. Everyone was frustrated.

I was riding Tony's bicycle, and one guy asked to borrow it. They were there helping us; I couldn't exactly say no. Time kept ticking. Like forty minutes later, he came back. Tony asked for his bike back when Twist put his hand on it, saying, 'This is my bike.'

Tony replied, 'No, it's not; it's mine.' So he tried to grab it back, but a fight broke out. This wasn't good.

Tony fought back, as he was only defending his property, at which point all hell broke loose. Twist pulled out a knife, looked at it, and then threw it on the floor. Within seconds, a few boys jumped Tony, and Ceas pulled out a hammer and hit Tony in the mouth twice. Damon and Anthony jumped in to help, but we were clearly outnumbered. A skip was close by, and many ran and got weapons. Someone used their motorcycle helmet and hit Damon's head multiple times. I thought it'd be stupid to fight back as we couldn't win, so I yelled, 'Stop' while trying to push them off him. I got punched in the head from behind.

It was mostly Damon and Anthony getting hit, as Tony was already down, and the others must've thought like me, so they just stood there shocked. It burned my soul to see Damon getting hurt because he had gotten the worst of it. They were hitting him with big wooden sticks, punches, and kicks. Damon was a passionate big brother and would have gone to the ends of the earth to defend his comrades. Seeing him beaten up in front of me was heartbreaking, knowing I couldn't help. There were at least five guys to one, so Damon and Anthony didn't stand a chance, but they fought as best they could and didn't give up.

Mum soon heard and came out screaming and shouting, 'Get off my son.' Then her boyfriend, Andrew, ran inside and returned with two large kitchen knives. He was small, roughly 5ft 6, but he did his best. A few neighbours came out of their houses, looking shocked. The Tulse Hill boys had done enough damage, so they retreated towards the estate. A few of my friends had run toward the top of the street in the other direction. I looked at Damon, and his eyes had literally changed colour. Whatever damage had been done to his head changed his eyes from green to bright grey, and he also threw up.

I ran up the road to find the rest of our boys there and told them to come back down. Tony was holding his face with blood in his mouth. His two top front teeth were missing, knocked out by the hammer. He was very distraught. 'What the fuck happened? I thought they were meant to be your friends?' I was speechless.

An ambulance arrived as we got back to our house. And just as this happened, our original opponents turned up in a car. At that point, the last boys from Tulse Hill Estate were walking off. Ceas recognised them, saying, 'They're there; we just smacked them up!' Noticing the emergency services on the scene, Flint didn't hang around. He made eye contact and then drove off.

This was the worst day of my life; it all happened so fast. What a disaster. I felt so guilty because it was my idea to get these guys to help in the first place, and I didn't join in the fight. And I lent the guy Tony's bike. It was always me. I just knew we couldn't win. Hitting back couldn't have helped much. It had happened, and I couldn't change that. So much for relying on people that you aren't really close with.

The ambulance checked Damon over and suggested he go to the hospital to get adequately assessed, but he didn't go. And the rest of our boys soon went home. Damon had a few bruises on his head, a badly swollen hand and a black eye. He wasn't in great shape, but he could function. That evening Flint called and said he still wanted the money or there'd be more trouble. So, after a brief discussion, Damon decided it was easier to just pay him.

They chose a meeting point, Streatham High-street. Damon picked this spot because it was safer, with many witnesses, out in the open. The next day, he got the money, and the meeting time approached. I offered to go with him, but he thought it'd be better to go with just Andrew, as he was an adult, and Damon never wanted it to seem like he wanted trouble.

A few hours passed, and they hadn't returned. Andrew then turned up alone, stating that Damon paid Flint the money whilst he watched from across the street. Some boys turned up, and once he had paid, one punched him, so he ran without pursuit. His hand hurt even more, so he went to the hospital. Poor Damon had barely recovered and was hurt again. All over one hundred pounds, which he eventually paid anyway. In hindsight, it would've been easier to have just paid originally.

Damon returned later that night with his hand in a cast. His hand was fractured the day before, but he never knew because he hadn't gone to the hospital. He was in even worse shape than before, but he was a soldier and took it all like a man. I felt incredibly sorry for him; he'd been through so much. Why was it always him who got the worst of it? Damon always seemed to get the short end of the stick.

Inside I felt like a right wimp. At every opportunity, I always took the easy route, from the Itchy situation to running away in Pimlico and this time not fighting back. I tried to avoid fighting; it was never my thing. Who'd enjoy being physically hurt, as that's usually the outcome? I was generally tough and streetwise, but I never liked fighting deep down. Over the next few days, Damon took things easy. He couldn't ride his moped because of his fractured hand, so it ended up just sitting in our garden.

The summer holidays soon ended, and I entered my last school year. I wore a black blazer instead of burgundy, which was a relief because people couldn't tell which school I was from, as many schools' uniforms were black blazers. However, my attendance was still terrible, and sometimes I'd get there literally just before lunchtime. Classmates laughed when I strolled in halfway through the day. On P.E. days, sometimes, I'd arrive, have lunch, and then go home, disappearing when boarding our school bus for P.E.

13

Final School Days

One morning, when Damon wasn't around for a few days, I decided I wanted to impress my school friends, so I took his moped to ride to school. I circled the block once for practice, as I'd never ridden one before, but I figured it couldn't be too difficult. Once I'd done that successfully, I felt ready.

I was at the end of my road, and when the light hit green, I pulled the throttle. But it went faster than I expected, and I couldn't let go of it. Within a second, I crashed into the phone box opposite my road. I was ok, but the bike's front panels were broken, and half had fallen off. What an embarrassment. 'Are you alright?' a woman asked.

'I'm fine, thanks.' But the bike definitely wasn't. I wheeled it back home, thinking what an idiot I was for crashing. And how I'd let my brother down even more with this doing.

I put the bike in the garden, covered it, and thought I'd get the bus to school and deal with it later. I couldn't focus all day, mentally replaying what'd happened, thinking how stupid I was. 'Why didn't you first go around the block a few more times?' I repeated. When school finished, I bought duct tape and rushed home. I put the broken panel bits back on and taped them all up, but it was far from the same bike as before. It looked feeble, all stuck together with black tape. It still worked but was nowhere near as presentable. When Damon returned, I told him; surprisingly, he wasn't that mad. He seemed different. Maybe enough dramas had occurred, and he just wanted a simpler life.

A few weeks later, Aaron came around when Damon was out, so we took the moped to Pollards Hill. We met up with his friends, and one owned a Gilera Runner. We raced around the streets for hours; Aaron rode with me on the back. I also practised myself and figured it out. I rode fine without crashing by the day's end. It was a fun day out racing, with Aaron driving me home that night.

I tried riding to school again a few days later, and this time, I made it. I never knew the highway code, so I went through a red light but wasn't seen by any police. Finally arriving, I felt like a champion because only one other guy in my year rode one to school. My mates laughed at its terrible state, but at least I had one to ride.

I noticed the petrol sign bleeping on my way home, so I pulled into a petrol station. I had fifty pence, so I went to the pump. I never knew what petrol it took. Leaded gasoline, unleaded, or diesel? I was going to ask someone, but my pride to not look stupid thought, fuck it, they can't be that different. So I put diesel in, paid, and rode home.

A few days later, it wouldn't start. I rang Aaron and asked him a few questions, mentioning the petrol I put in. 'That's the wrong petrol, Dupz. You've probably broken it. You'll have to drain the engine, which costs like two hundred pounds.' But, of course, I was broke, so I couldn't afford it. I felt like even more of an idiot. After all the problems Damon suffered acquiring that bike for me to ride it, crash it, put in the wrong petrol, and break it, what a muppet.

I attended many house parties, raves, and bars around this age. I'd regularly meet up with some Tulse Hill boys, and we'd all roll out together. They weren't the ones we fought; most were older, but sometimes some we fought came. That fight was in the past; I didn't keep a grudge; life went on.

Damon spent a lot of time in Pimlico with Michelle, and I'd hang out there sometimes, still avoiding that one guy. This was when I met an eighteen-year-old girl called Sam. 'Do you remember me?' she said, reminding me that she was the girl I spoke to on the phone when I was young. Yes, I remember you, but I'm not a little kid anymore, that's for sure.

I went to hers, and she'd just come out of an unhealthy relationship. Her ex-boyfriend was twenty-one and a hench, with a superbike. He locked her in the house, made her not wear makeup, and dressed her down. She didn't have to worry about that with me. We hit it off straight away, soon becoming an item. She had a full-time job as a secretary, so she had more money than me, a schoolboy.

It was a magical time; I felt like a real G, having a grown-up girlfriend. We soon slept together; this was my first proper adult relationship. I met her at work sometimes, and her colleague playfully mocked her upon seeing me in school uniform. Then, one evening, we returned to her office and had sex on the boardroom table, finishing five minutes before the overnight cleaner arrived. That was close, like out of a movie. I loved being in a mature relationship, and every exciting moment nourished my urge for adventure.

I was a young man and soon came my sixteenth. Sam spent fifteen hours drawing me a perfect picture of *Dragon Ball Z's* Goku on a birthday card; it was exceptional. Having a proper relationship was fun. Being three years older, Sam taught me certain things about adult life. Mum still drank and smoked but was good at keeping it from our eyes as much as possible; she never smoked in front of us.

Social services soon got involved because Mum had Tyreese, still a baby. They discussed taking him into foster care, so we spoke with Debbie, Michelle's mum, and she took him instead. That was better, as he was still technically with us - with trusted, good people. Mum cried seeing him go but knew it was best.

Christmas 2003 came, and after a little celebration at home with Mum, Damon and I walked the hour to Michelle's, as no busses ran on Christmas day. Sam, who grew up with her, met us there, and we had a great day with a lovely dinner. The following year, Sam, renting an expensive room, realized our spare room was cheaper, so she moved in.

We redecorated and carpeted it and moved all her stuff in. She had nice things: a fifteen hundred pound 32inch Sony TV with surround sound; her room looked great. After a while, Sam disputed the rent. She was my girlfriend;

I mostly slept in her room, so why should she pay full rent? Mum squashed it but said she must contribute and pay her way.

I still loved making music, and I was talented at it. Damon, Michelle, and I created a song, performed it in her local church competition, and won. I was very into Jesus, maybe over-obsessed, as I put religion before almost anything, even logic. I sometimes chose what was right in the religious view over what my brain told me was logically correct.

This was a concerning way to be. I repeatedly said the Lord's Prayer in my head, thinking I was showing God my devotion. I now know that this wasn't a genuine connection with our creator. Many people experience like-minded unhealthy over-religiousness. I've always been a perfectionist, so I give my best whenever I do something. I won't stop until I achieve the perfect outcome. I applied this to everything, including religion, so it was all or nothing.

Sam and I soon started arguing, so she decided to take a break after roughly five months. We still shared a bed, as it was the only room we had, but we were definitely over. This was difficult for me because I still loved her. I fell in love with her after only a few days. Looking back, I told most girls I love them after four days or so of being with them twenty-four-seven. I must fall easily. We even took a romantic weekend trip to Wales but couldn't rekindle our flame. I wanted to, but the feelings seemed one way.

A song, 'Through the Wire,' by a new artist Kanye West, was playing on the radio in our cab back from the train station. I loved this song, I loved Sam, but she was no longer in love with me. I soon accepted it and tried to move on. Mum hated seeing me smitten by a girl who wasn't interested. We still lived together, so it wasn't easy.

I watched a movie called *In Hell*, with Jean Claude Van Damme, where he goes to a Russian prison. A young American guy unfairly also ends up there and gets raped and murdered. This affected my mentality; from that day, I was no longer the little guy. I started working out obsessively, maybe using it to harness all the emotions of breaking up. I was pretty ripped within a few months and became a slight fitness freak, trying to get all my friends in on it.

Sam turned nineteen, and it then came time for my GCSE exams. I wasn't expecting excellent grades, as I attended school less than half the time. One night, Trula stayed over until 3am, and I missed a math exam the next day, contributing 40% to the final grade. I did hardly any coursework and still got a decent E in maths. I achieved six A to C passes, so I did reasonably OK. I'd finally finished secondary school.

14

College

We had a friend called Sarah, a twenty-three-year-old mixed-race girl who was like a big sister to us. She got me a weekend job helping her sell things at Blue Orchid nightclub in Croydon. I got fifteen pounds, plus a free night out. If asked, I'd say I was eighteen - the age for entrance. There were so many sexy girls around I didn't know what to do. We sold glow sticks, roses, and many other things to enhance a night out.

I was still religious and a little introverted, so I never took advantage of all the pretty girls available. All I really wanted was a beautiful girl of my own. Sarah's ex-boyfriend was also one of the head bouncers at Caesar's in Streatham and was 6ft. 4, with a body like Hercules. So, we also did the odd work there, with free drinks all night. Many people got drunk, and we witnessed a few crazy incidents.

We met Uncle Denny's son, Echo, who was twenty-three and had a superbike and Lexus car. We met his cousins, who we also considered cousins. They had a professional music studio and also made music. We soon created a music group, *Black Ice*, and worked together, performing once in a west London club.

Sam's dad, Larry, was a nice quiet man who'd recently sold his house and started renting our spare room. He was the only family Sam had, as her mother passed away when she was young. After selling his home, Larry had a lot of money and went on many holidays. He took Mum on two and Sam on more, but he soon relapsed into alcoholism. He drank vodka neat like water.

Once, Michelle and I switched it with water to see if he noticed. He didn't and thought it was vodka, saying it tasted nice. That made us giggle. He was humble and caring and listened to Van Morrison's music all day. 'Van the man,' he called him; I heard it so much that I started liking it too; it was relaxing. Mum was also pregnant again. This was great; Mum desperately wanted a girl, as she already had four boys. We hoped that God would give us a sister.

Summer soon came, and Larry bought ten tickets for a two-week all-inclusive holiday to Cancun, Mexico. Unfortunately, Damon and Michelle pulled out at the last moment because they had college exams. So Sam and I went through her phone, wondering whether to start at a or z, asking people if they wanted a free holiday. She eventually settled on her two friends, Chris and Kenny, who were overjoyed at the opportunity.

Ten of us, including Sam's old best male friend Tariq, Uncle Denny, Tina, Mum, Larry, and Sam all landed in Mexico for an exciting holiday adventure. The sun wasn't shining upon arrival, so Tina decided to sunbathe without sunscreen. The next day, she was in terrible pain, burnt all over, with her skin literally peeling. 'I didn't know you could get burnt when the bloody sun wasn't even shining.' This ruined the first week of her holiday as she stayed in her room and missed out on all the fun things we did together.

We visited Mexico City, did snorkelling, rode jet skis, got massages, and had a great time. Every day there were people selling weed and stuff on the beach. Uncle Denny also got arrested, and we paid to bail him out. The jail at the police station didn't look nice; it was a concrete surface to sleep on with a toilet.

We met some friendly young American people, but they spoke with the others more. I was still very religious, and I see this was negative in hindsight. For years, my over-religious attitude kept me introverted and must've scared people off. Because I remember getting a funny vibe, as people probably thought I was some weird over-religious guy. To a degree, I was.

A relationship with God is beautiful, but being strictly religious differs significantly from a healthy relationship with our creator. I'd walk around holding my cross around my neck in my hand, making the cross sign at inappropriate times. Our holiday in Mexico ended after two crazy, fun-filled weeks. We returned to tell Damon and Michelle about the incredible experience they'd missed.

I was still besotted with Sam but discovered she'd slept with Chris in Mexico. This hurt because she was my first love; I loved her still and hoped we'd rekindle. I introduced my local friend Jason to Sam, who said he looked like a little girl and was pretty. He was two years younger than me and was one of my best friends. We'd listen to music from PDC, Tempman, and the Roadside Geez, to name a few, and our American favourites.

These were the days of *Grand Theft Auto-Vice City*, which we played for hours. Jason's older cousins, who I respected, came around for epic battles on *Street Fighter*. His cousin Leon was nineteen and got loads of girls' attention. Sam fancied him, but her efforts were unsuccessful as he wasn't into white girls. Once, I started a flour fight, throwing it right in Sam's face. Jason didn't want to get hit, but he got it too, at which point everyone, including Mum, joined in. I recommend trying this at least once; it was worth the cleaning.

Sam and Jason clicked. It never took long to realize that she fancied him, and they soon became an item. This was hell for me; my little best friend, who wasn't even fifteen, was in front of me in my own house, making out with the girl I was still obsessed with. It was a hard pill to swallow.

His cousins could see my despair, 'Oi Duppy, it must burn you seeing Jason kissing your girl, rude boy? In your own house as well.'

'Yeah, it does, but what can I do?'

"Boy, that could never happen in my yard, fam; you must be mad,' they mocked. I had to accept it and carry on, but it hurt inside. It eventually became too uncomfortable, Jason talking about sex, so Sam found a flat to rent in Leyton, East London. She moved out, and he spent most of that summer holiday with her. I regularly visited, but witnessing them as a couple wasn't easy because I still had feelings for my first adult girlfriend.

My stepdad, Clive, gave me some work helping him as a plumber's mate, which I did here and there but didn't stick to. It was fun being with him, and he sometimes took me to a bar after work. Tyreese was also put into foster care with a family in Brixton, which wasn't great. Still, they were friendly, and we could visit him regularly.

September soon arrived, and I'd been accepted into Westminster Kingsway College on a two-year music production course. This was great because it was a college only for performing arts. There were also many pretty girls, and a guy in the eighty-percent female acting class said, 'Bro, almost every girl in my class fancies you.' I'd never felt so lucky.

I fancied Gabby, the prettiest girl in college in my eyes. But I was still very religious. So once again, my crazy over religiousness significantly prevented me from getting my desire. One girl told me that someone fancied me; I'm sure she meant Gabby, but I never asked her who, saying, 'What's meant to be, will be. I don't wanna know who fancies me.' But really, I did; I even told friends about her. Looking back, I realise we grow extremely wiser with age, and back then, I hardly knew myself.

A blind boy from college took me to a Jill Scott concert at Brixton Academy. My first concert was exciting. When I walked around Brixton with him holding my arm, we got a few funny stares. They probably thought we were homosexual, but most eventually noticed he was blind. I met some lovely people at college, including a girl named Tia and another called Eliza.

On the 11th of October 2004, our prayers were answered, and Mum gave birth to our little sister. We discussed names, and Damon liked Sky. After my college friend and a childhood favourite Nickelodeon program *Sister Sister*, I suggested Tia or Tiana. One of the twins in it was called Tia. Mum chose Tiana, which sounded great with Tyreese. They share the same initials, T.A.R. This time, though, Tiana was taken straight from the hospital after a few days to the same family as Tyreese. At least they were together, and we could see them. This was heartbreaking for Mum. She cried but knew it was best.

On the 30thof October 2004, David Morley was killed by a group of teenagers doing happy slapping. One of the four eventually found guilty, who got twelve years in prison, was my friend from Kennington, David Blenman, or Jynx. He was more Mousy's mate but was still a pal. I was shocked to see him in a national news report for murder, the most heinous crime. It's atrocious what youth do for kicks; to them, it's fun, but for the victim, it's hell.

Once locally, we went out looking for drama. We spotted a man walking, and six of us jumped him. We grabbed his bag while he pleaded, 'Please, I'll give you money,' but we weren't paying attention. Like frenzied hyenas, drunk off our prey, we grabbed his rucksack, and two of my friends hit his head with bottles, one smashed. We emptied the backpack at home to find two slipknot hoodies of no value to us. He offered money, yet we never took it. Wasn't that the aim of a robbery? It showed how mindless and barbaric youth can sometimes be without considering their victim's feelings.

When young, I thought of the world as a physical phenomenon based on separateness. I never saw others as a part of myself. They were them, and I was me, not connected. I was wrong. Science proves that we're all interconnected, all fabrics of the same reality.

15

The Problems Really Start

My seventeenth birthday arrived, and I held a party. All my friends came, plus Tia and Eliza from college; it was great. Everyone loved the main attraction, Mum, the party's life, dancing away. It was a lot quieter than the last party I held.

Patrick, Mum's cool Jamaican friend, was always at ours. 'My friend wants me to paint his house. You wanna help me, Danny, forty pounds a day?' The guy would give us a half-ounce of weed for the other two days' work. I ended up doing this with him, and because I was still very into weed, I stupidly put this before college and dropped out.

I soon attended the job centre and applied for a job in a nursery, which coincidentally was at the end of my road. On my first day, they left me alone with the toddlers. I was shocked because there wasn't enough time to do police checks on me. I could've been a wrong-un, and they wouldn't have known. Thankfully, I'm a good guy. My first week's wages were about one-hundred-and-seventy pounds after tax. Not much, but the first decent bit of money I'd ever earned. It felt terrific coming home, knowing I'd made it legitimately. Then my job at the nursery ended after two weeks. They found someone more qualified for the position and said they didn't need me anymore. I had no idea what to do.

One morning, I woke to find my laptop missing. I had a little padlock on my studio door and locked it at night, but that night I'd forgotten. I asked

Mum who had been in the house, and she said it was mainly just her and Uncle Denny. I investigated, but my laptop was already gone. Probably sold for crack. Uncle Denny crossed my mind because he acted slightly suspiciously. But he cared for us a lot. He was the leading supporter of my music, as he also had a minor music career when he was young. I was upset that every song I'd created was gone. This was soul-destroying, as it completely changed my music dreams' reality. And who knew where music could've taken me? Once, I saw the rapper Big Narstie waiting outside the Brixton Housing office. It just shows many successful people have humble beginnings.

Mum's friend Patrick soon told me that the guy whose house we painted, a yardie called Doggie, had shown him a gun and said he'd recently robbed a man for an ounce of coke. We joked about how long it'd take us to smoke an ounce. A few weeks later, Patrick said Doggie was interested in buying a nine-bar: nine ounces of weed. He asked if I knew of anyone to get it from.

I spoke with Jason's cousin Mark, my age and my new best friend since Jason got with Sam. He knew Blacka, who lived locally in Damon's ex Sarah's old house since they'd moved out. Mark phoned and told him what we needed. We knew that we'd earn some weed from this deal. Blacka asked if we had the money, and Doggie showed us a handful of cash earlier, so we knew he had it. It was around one thousand pounds, and Doggie complained, asking for it cheaper.

Blacka arrived with the most enormous bag of weed I'd ever seen. We took a few pictures holding it as a keepsake. Then, we rang Doggie, who took ages, making Blacka paranoid. Finally, he arrived with a friend, and Blacka tried to make the deal. Doggie showed us the money but said he wanted to ensure it was the correct nine ounces. Blacka never liked this; he assured us he had weighed it twice. 'Go back to mine and make sure it's on point,' Doggie said, passing me his keys. So, Blacka and I went to Doggie's.

We'd weighed it all correctly, and then Doggie and his friend entered. He pulled out a big handgun and stuck it in Blacka's face. He didn't have to say much; we knew what was happening. Blacka raised his hands and said, 'Please don't shoot me. I'm only fifteen.' Doggie took the weed, and Blacka darted out the front door with me close behind. This was bad.

I ran home and told Mark. 'Argh, Duppy man, how could you let this happen? I knew something wasn't right.' He'd contacted Blacka, so he'd also get blamed. We abruptly left my house because we knew we'd face swift retribution. We didn't know where to go, so we silenced our phones and rushed back to Doggie's flat. I still had the front door key, so we went inside, but it was empty. We then hid in a bush on the next street to mine.

Blacka rang, screaming down the phone, 'You robbed me.' We apologized and tried to convince him that we weren't behind this. But he wasn't hearing it and said that trouble was coming our way. Mark was distraught. Mum soon rang me, saying Blacka and a few others were going crazy at my door. I felt terrible hearing the desperation in her voice. I put Mum and Damon in that position, and I couldn't help them. We couldn't go back as we'd get a beating. So, we stayed in the bush for an hour, and then both went home. What a disaster.

I returned to Doggie's the next day, but he'd already changed the locks. So I rang him but got no answer. Then, finally, when I called from a different number, he answered, and I remember his words as they've haunted me, "You no learn yet nigger?"

I told Patrick, and he was a little un-shocked. 'Doggie is a gunman and robber; you should've been more careful, Danny. He robbed a dealer for an ounce of coke just the other day. I told you this already.' I recalled what he said before; I wish I'd initially paid more attention. Blaming Patrick for sending Doggie my way wouldn't have helped; I was already stuck in the mud.

I eventually spoke to Blacka, who told me the debt was on me. I understood street politics, so I realized my best option was to pay for what he had lost. I asked Mark if he could contribute, but he lived in Thornton Heath and Blacka didn't know where, so he wasn't in the firing line. 'Duppy, I was just the middleman. This was your fault; I ain't paying anything.'

Two days after the robbery, I went to Doggie's flat and broke the kitchen window with a rock. I left it for an hour, and when no police arrived, I returned and opened the window by putting my hand through the hole. I wanted to take all and anything worth money. He had hardly anything valuable except a huge TV and a PlayStation 2, so I grabbed the PS2 and left. I was a little scared as I'd robbed a gunman's flat and knew I'd be his first suspect.

I told Blacka what I'd done to show I was trying and offered him the PlayStation 2, but he didn't want it as he already had two. He just wanted his money and said I owed him one thousand pounds. I sold the PlayStation, but after getting only forty pounds, I realized this was too little to give to Blacka and just bought weed to destress myself. This was a huge problem. Where was I going to get a grand from? I could hardly afford a ten-pound bag of weed.

I stopped going out, and because Blacka probably thought of my house like a crack house, it luckily scared him off slightly. I was really depressed and went into my shell. I stayed inside for months, thinking of ways to fix this situation. Finally, one of our lodgers paid three hundred pounds monthly and, thankfully, Mum let me use it once to pay Blacka. I met him with Damon and gave him the money, assuring him I was sorry and it wasn't intentional. I believe he knew this because I had to pay for what was stolen. He wasn't happy, but he took it and said he wanted the rest soon.

Around my local area, I'd recently befriended a Jamaican boy named Tam-Tam. He was only fourteen but had a big beard and was a real little badman. He was notorious locally, and no one messed with him. He began spending a lot of time at my house, bunking off from the centre he went to for those kicked out of regular school. We'd smoke weed and listen to rap music. He introduced me to a few local boys like Younger Crafty and his younger cousin, Pun.

Mum had split from Andrew and was dating a fellow drinker named Glenn, Crafty's uncle, coincidently. I got on well with these guys, who were notorious in the streets, which I liked. Everybody wants well-respected friends. Damon wasn't too fond of them, as he had a full-time job and had given up street life completely. They were cool, but there was tension now and then. We were mates, but I knew that my house, which they could hang out in, was also a factor in their frequenting.

I then discovered Tyreese and Tiana had left the UK to go and live with their grandma in Jamaica. It was sad that we wouldn't see them anymore, but I was delighted they were with family who would care for them correctly. Damon also soon broke up with Michelle.

Tam–Tam once brought two young girls from Epson round who ended up staying for a few days; one called Lucy was very pretty. Tam liked her, but she did things with Mark and others. We never told him because he would've been quite upset. One day Mum's friend, Patrick, asked me to hold on to an eighth of crack he was selling. He gave it to me to keep it safe, as I didn't smoke it. And as he smoked, he thought he might smoke it off if in his possession.

I was depressed and alone in my room with around thirty rocks, thinking what do Mum and all these people love so much about this stuff? What have I got to lose? I might as well try it; it's only a one-off. Yeah, once can't hurt. If I had only known then how much this choice would affect my life. I found a plastic bottle, burnt a hole, and put some foil on top. I put holes in the foil, opened a rock, and put some straight on. I didn't want anyone to hear the lighter, so I lit a candle and burnt newspaper as my flame. I smoked.

The crack crackled as I inhaled, and the bottle filled with smoke. I felt a rush like I'd never felt before. My whole body tingled, and I got a lovely warm feeling. It felt nice. I did another pipe and got that rush again, but the first one was more intense. So I opened another rock and smoked that too. Then another.

Knock, knock, knock. 'Danny, Danny boy, open the door, please. I need my things.' Oh no, Patrick wanted his stuff! What do I do? He's gonna be mad at me for smoking some. I'll not answer and pretend I'm asleep. My door was locked, so he couldn't get in.

Knock, knock, knock, 'Danny, open the door.' There was frustration in his voice. He knocked for a few minutes; he knew something was wrong.

He called Mum, who also knocked. 'Dan, Dan. He's probably asleep, Patrick.' Bang, bang, bang.

'Something is up, Lu-Lu; he must be smoking?'

'No, Daniel doesn't smoke. He wouldn't do that. Give him some time; he'll probably wake up soon.'

'Mcheeew, bomboclart him a take the piss.' And the knocking stopped. Oh no, what was I to do? How was I gonna get myself out of this one?

I left it for a few hours, then eventually came out. Patrick looked frustrated sitting in the front room. I gave him his parcel, 'Patrick, I'm sorry, I smoked three.'

'Danny, why did you do that? Smoking isn't good. What did you smoke it on?' I went and got the pipe. "Where is the ash?"

"What ash?"

"You didn't use ash, Danny? Rassclart, you ah waste the ting. You must put ash on top of the pipe. You mash up my profit; I might as well smoke it now.'

Patrick sorted out the pipe correctly and then smoked some himself. 'Can I have one, please?'

'No, Danny, this stuff is not good. It's very addictive, don't do it.'

'I've already done three; it doesn't make a difference now. Please don't leave me out.'

He put some on for me, and I smoked it correctly this time. It was much better with cigarette ash on it. The buzz was twice as good, and we smoked a few rocks together. Luckily, Mum wasn't home because she'd be furious, knowing I'd tried crack. Patrick asked if I knew any girls who smoked, but I didn't, so he left to find one to smoke with instead. I wanted him to smoke more with me, but beggars cannot be choosers. I was officially a crack smoker.

After a few weeks, Mum got suspicious of my behaviour, so I confessed I had been smoking. She was distraught and said she wouldn't be giving me any. So, when Mum was out and smokers came round, I'd let them in and they'd share with me. Some were hesitant because I was young, but when I said they must leave if they didn't share, most eventually folded. The odd person left and took their drugs with them.

The next few months were a drama because I lusted for crack; it became my main priority. I looked forward to smoking it whenever possible and was always trying to find ways to acquire it. It's true; it feels so good that you can't stop once you pop. Mum was heartbroken that I'd started smoking but said if I was doing it, she'd prefer I did it around her where she knew I was safe. Better than out on the streets without her protection.

I'd always annoy Mum and her friends, getting the odd pipe here and there. I bugged them when they smoked until they gave in. After that, I drifted away from my friends and still had the drama of owing Blacka money, so I mostly stayed inside, seeking a free smoke. Tam-Tam and his mates still visited, but my friends lost respect for me as I smoked crack, the one thing we all said we'd never do.

Our front door was weak from being forced open repeatedly; Tam-Tam knew this. So I came home a few times to find him and a gang of other young boys sitting in my front room. When I asked how he got in, he muttered a story saying someone let him in; but I believed he'd just forced the door. Once, he knocked a few times, but I didn't answer, so he barged it open. He was shocked to see me home and diverted the fact he'd barged the door by questioning why I didn't open it. But hey, it proved my belief.

He also thought this was an opportunity for him to make money. So, he bought half a sixteenth of white, which isn't much - something we could get for forty pounds and smoke in one sitting - and he cut it up into ten little rocks. It was weak, but he expected me to entice smokers into buying it. But then they'd be buying crap; how would that benefit me when I relied on them for a free smoke? So, I told them to buy from legitimate dealers, and he didn't like it. I explained my reasoning, but he thought crack was crack and smokers should buy whatever he offered. Youngsters' mentality is astonishing.

16

Crack Takes Over

One day I argued with Mum and said, 'I wish you were dead.' Words someone should never say. Of course, I never meant it, but Mum replied, 'Be careful what you wish for. I'll be gone one day, and what will you do then?'

That very night I was walking up Brixton Hill when I heard someone painfully yell; it sounded like Mum. I walked towards the groaning, and to my surprise, it was Mum - upside down, with her head still on the floor. She'd just drunkenly fallen off a pub bench and hit her head. It bled terribly, and a huge bump an inch across appeared immediately; I felt so sorry for her. I called an ambulance, but they said they were overwhelmed, so we got the bus to Kings College hospital.

We sought help upon arrival, but Mum was still drunk, and the staff were very un-empathetic. 'You lesbian,' Mum called a rude nurse, who then said we must leave. I was surprised and angry because Mum clearly needed stitches. But the nurse's eyes showed her pleasure in kicking us out.

I half begged them to treat her, 'Don't you have a system where you can help someone who needs medical attention, even if they're slightly unruly?' But no, they stated Mum was abusive, so she must leave. I felt sickened.

Mum was a Spartan, 'Fuck it. Let's get a pipe; that'll take the pain away.' So we went home, bought a twenty-pound rock, and I cleaned her wound myself.

She awoke the next day with a headache, 'Mum, please go to the hospital.'

'Nah, don't worry about me; I'll be alright; I'm a soldier.' To this day, I feel terrible about what I said that previous evening. What a coincidence that I said those nasty words and then walked past the moment Mum hurt herself. That got me wondering how powerful our words may indeed be.

Mum got us an Xbox for Christmas, which we enjoyed very much because we no longer had a PlayStation 2. Then, in late January, Tam-Tam and K-Dogg knocked on the door. K-Dogg was notorious for bullying and robbing anyone he could victimize; we weren't fond of him. Tam-Tam barged past me into my front room, and I was shocked and confused.

I entered to find him unplugging our Xbox. 'Damon, quick,' I shout.

It all happened so fast, and as we tried to stop Tam-Tam from leaving, K-Dogg pulled a gun under his t-shirt and pointed it, saying, 'Mind I burst you; mind I burst you.' Tam-Tam and Crafty had shown me guns before, so I knew this was serious.

Not wanting to get shot, we let them leave. I was so upset. Not because we lost the computer, but because it was a Christmas gift from Mum. She always said, 'You only get one mum,' and boy is that true. We were also disappointed with Tam because he was a close friend, so his actions surprised us.

He and Mum had a unique friendship, as their birthdays were only two days apart, so both Virgo's. After a few weeks, I think Tam-Tam robbed someone else for a PlayStation 2 because he gifted us one, apologizing for stealing our Xbox. He was desperate for some weed that day, so he decided to rob and sell our console, as I later found out.

We also had a new lodger called Ricky, a prolific crack-smoking burglar. Every day, he stole from like nine till five and once overslept, complaining, 'Daniel, why didn't you wake me up for work?' He went around when people were out working and rang their doorbell. If no one answered, he'd find a way through a door or window. He'd stack the goods, sometimes in their front garden, then call a cab to come and collect them.

Soon after he moved in, I heard reports that many neighbours had recently been robbed. The police knocked on our door, 'There's been a string of burglaries on your street, be cautious.' If they only knew. He sold stolen items to local shops, the chip shop being his favourite. The numerous goods he came home with were crazy; he even had a stolen Mini Cooper parked outside.

On my road, a house had a sign in its window stating, 'I was recently burgled, and my Apple Mac laptop was stolen. I don't care about anything else, but that contained many irreplaceable important files. I'll pay six hundred pounds if it's returned. I won't involve the police.' So I told Ricky, but he'd sold it to the chip shop for £120. He considered repurchasing it to resell to its owner for the extra 480. But he thought it'd be risky, and they'd maybe involve the police. I felt sorry for this person as I could relate to losing a priceless laptop.

Mum soon had a new boyfriend, an Italian chef named Steff. Many female drug users used prostitution for money, and Mum had also done this over the years. I never viewed Mum as a prostitute, but she used it sometimes to make fast bucks. She was great at grafting money and would go out at night and come back twenty minutes later with sixty pounds, saying it took her five minutes to make.

Mum never went into detail as she had decorum and high self-respect but said she rarely slept with them. Instead, she'd hustle and graft them, doing as little as possible to accomplish her goal. She joked once about giving a man a two-minute hand job, and the mission was complete. Sometimes, Mum brought men home but was very private and didn't disturb us. Some turned and ran when they walked through the door and saw Damon or me. Sometimes, Mum would come back without any luck, saying, 'It was dead out there.'

Brixton Hill was notorious for prostitution; women walked up and down every night, getting picked up in cars. I never lost an ounce of respect for Mum because she was a genuine connoisseur of the streets. She grafted her money with as much dignity as a woman could possess. She was a hustler, and working the streets for money was what most drug users did; they've got to source money somewhere.

Crack is more psychologically addictive than physical, so I didn't smoke it all the time. I couldn't afford it. I still hung out with my friends. I didn't have to pay for weed because my mates usually saved me some spliff, and I didn't need much to get high because I smoked it less now.

We'd smoke and watch the latest UK grime DVDs with our favourite artists, Roadside Geez, PDC, and SMS. They were local artists from south London, mainly Brixton. R.A: Real Artillery was my favourite, as he authentically rapped about street life and lived what he preached. I'm sure I'd walked past him a few times. We also loved the emcees from East London, some of the original founders of grime music. We enjoyed 'Lord of The Mics,' which inspired us.

I also discovered that I could get money for free from the Jobcentre by signing on, which I soon did. When my claim was live, I applied for a loan and eventually received £435. I called Blacka immediately, met and gave him four hundred pounds. I was stressed because I knew I was giving it away for nothing, all for a mistake.

I bought myself a twenty-pound rock, some food and tobacco with the rest. I'd paid seven hundred by then - most of the one thousand pounds I owed and thought that's all he's getting; I ain't paying more. I also heard through the grapevine that Blacka's mum, who was well-respected, found out who Doggy was and got back the money. It wasn't worth the trouble once Doggy realized he'd robbed someone whose family had serious affiliations, probably shooters. So, Blacka maybe eventually got more money than he initially required.

I also found Doggy in my house again months later. Ricky was cooking up crack for him in his room and asked if I had any ammonia or cleaning products to mix into it. I asked him if he'd give me anything, and he kept fobbing me off, saying, 'Later.' What a cheek, robbing me, then cooking up ounces in my house and giving me nothing; how disrespectful. I eventually smoked some, which was weak and had a funny cleaning product taste.

One evening there was a knock on the door, and Damon opened it. It was K-Dogg, highly shaken. 'Please let me in; we just shot Mover's hand off.' We were far from friends but recognized the severity of the situation. I didn't get involved, and because Damon was older, K-Dogg looked more to him for guidance. Damon sat him down in the front room and supported him, later telling me everything. K-Dogg, Ceas, and Mover had tried to rob someone locally with a shotgun. Unfortunately, its light trigger was accidentally squeezed, hitting their own team. I think K-Dogg said Ceas was responsible. What a crazy experience that must've been!

I soon turned eighteen and was officially an adult. Unfortunately, I didn't keep up with the job centre's requirements, so my benefits stopped after literally one payment. Damon had also had enough of all the dramas. At nineteen, he moved out, renting a room from Mum's friend, Paul. He was only a few minutes away at the end of our street and across the road on Jebb Avenue, which was great as he was still close by.

It was then just Mum and me at home. Nothing changed much, but it got a little more hectic. Mum spent most of her time with her partner, Steff, who earned good money, sometimes three to five hundred pounds a night. They smoked a lot together, with me nagging for some. Steff didn't like giving me any crack. So, Mum would nick bits off him when he wasn't looking and pass them to me slyly. Mum also had her best friend, Clive, who'd visit and never gave me any either. The dramas always revolved around smoking.

A kind prostitute named Gemma visited regularly and worked the streets while six months pregnant. Then, another prostitute got murdered, with her throat slit and her body left in a wheelie bin. Mum eventually thought life would be easier to start afresh. We had rent arrears, noise complaints, Tam-Tam always here - and other issues - and Mum had had enough. So, Steff found them a one-bedroom flat in Pollards Hill. We were slightly upset about giving up a four-bedroom house as it was a valuable property, but to Mum, it seemed logical.

After roughly seven years, our adventures living on Brixton Hill were over. This left me homeless. I put some photos and all the precious belongings I'd gathered throughout my life into a single black bag and left it at Damon's. Ricky also packed his stuff and asked Damon to hold onto it. I got back in touch with my father, Everton, who said I could stay with him. When I went to collect my bag, Damon said no bags were left. 'Ricky came and took all of them.'

'Damon, one of those was mine. Can't you remember I left a bag here containing my entire life's belongings? They were precious, and you let him take them?' I tried contacting Ricky, but he was gone, and trying to get my stuff back proved unfruitful. Life goes on, as they say, but that troubled me.

17

Streatham Common/Vauxhall

This was my first time at my father's new flat; he had a lovely two-bedroom new build on Greyhound Lane in Streatham Common. I had my own room, and he always worked, so I was mostly there alone. 'This has your and Damon's name on it; you'll get this property when I'm gone,' he said.

I settled in, but he gave me an ultimatum. I was eighteen, a man, and my father wouldn't support me being a bum under his roof. 'Get a job within six months or leave.' I agreed and actively started looking for work. I also drastically cut down on smoking white as it was no longer around me, so I'd have to seek it out if I wanted some.

I soon made friends locally. A guy named Bruckie had a giant outhouse in his garden where we'd all hang out and smoke weed. I also introduced Jason, who was no longer with Sam, and Mark to my new friends. We hung out with two sets of brothers, who all looked up to an older boy named Acer with a superbike.

That summer was fun; a fresh start in a new area with new friends and some pretty girls. They never knew I smoked white, which I hardly did at the time, anyway. I wasn't around it and had no money, so I did it only once a month. I smoked weed daily and did something cheeky to attain it. My dad had numerous aftershave testers and big full bottles in my room. He was a security guard and got these from the malls he worked in. I swapped almost all of them with Brucky for weed and felt guilty because I knew Dad would eventually find out.

One night, I visited my mum at Paul's flat, where Damon lived. It was just me, Mum and Paul. Mum got a smoke, which she shared with me as usual. But I'd also smoked a weed spliff that night, as I knew being high on it enhanced the crack buzz. I was in the room with Mum; I smoked a pipe and then suddenly blacked out for a second. I had this powerful feeling that I knew God had been confirmed when I came to. Whatever happened to me completely changed my perspective. I felt like God was in the room with me, and I wanted to relay this feeling to the world. It was a scary emotion, but imagine feeling one hundred per cent that God is real. That's the closest description. That was another crucial moment that truly affected my life.

I started going crazy, making a lot of noise, and Paul came in. I jumped all over the house, proper on one, so he called the police. Next thing I started taking my clothes off. I couldn't help it; it wasn't through choice. It just felt like the correct thing to do at that moment. The police soon arrived, and they seemed puzzled. Five of them held me down; I had unprecedented strength. I don't know where it came from, but I've heard stories of people in drug-fuelled situations with superhuman strength.

Mum didn't want me arrested, and I did nothing illegal, so the police took me in the van to the hospital, half-naked. I awoke the next day with an embarrassing memory of the night before. I also felt that whatever I'd become called itself 'Whispers,' without knowing why. From that moment, my life was never the same. From then until the present, Whispers has been at the forefront of my mind, influencing my every thought. An experience where you feel one hundred percent that God is real and finding a tangible way to express that would change any sane person.

I returned to Paul's in hospital clothes, got my stuff, and went home. I also called Mum and apologized for acting crazy, asking her what had happened. She explained how I went nuts and that she told the police I needed help more than anything and not to arrest me. Thank you, Mum, my angel.

That summer, I heard a song, 'Free Yard,' on Channel U, the music channel with all the upcoming urban musical talent. Upon seeing the video, I was shocked to see Aggro, a guy I knew from the year below me at secondary school. He respected me and spat lyrics - sometimes when we had rap battles. How times had changed. I was happy for him and wished him success, but I knew this was where I should've been too. A friend from our previous music group Black Ice was also in the video. This reiterated that I could've been doing something similar.

A few weeks after my Whispers experience, I ended up at Damon's again, but it was just him and Steff there. I smoked a weed spliff before smoking a pipe again, and snap, I turned. I experienced the same feeling as before, knowing God was one hundred percent real. I went crazy again, but I was more familiar with it on my second experience. It felt like I had superpowers and was destined to save the universe from evil. I started stripping again and going nuts. Damon slapped me in the face dropping me to the floor, shaking me, saying, 'In Jesus' name, spirit come out of you.' I wriggled free and escaped out the front door.

I knew God was real and felt like I'd found a way to prove this; I had to show the world. I was wearing nothing but a t-shirt and was out on Brixton Hill naked from the waist down. I remember banging on the bus windows and walking in the middle of the road playing 'chicken' with an oncoming car. I didn't get too far before Damon and Steff came outside and brought me back.

When I returned to normal, I cheekily asked Damon, 'Who's Whispers?' They explained I was lucky to be alive as I almost got hit by a bus. It felt like I was a superhero, and this was my way to hone my powers. A few weeks later, Jason said, 'Oi Duppy, Tamer said she was on a bus and saw you walking the street naked; what's going on, fam?' Trying to explain this event was tricky.

After six months at Dad's, I hadn't gotten a job, so he said I must leave. I couldn't argue with him as he'd given me more than enough time. So I packed my bags, said goodbye, and left. Luckily Damon let me stay with him, but Paul only allowed me a few days, so Mum advised me to go to the housing council and not leave until they found me somewhere. I went there and to a few other agencies trying to get help. Because I was young with mental health issues, they deemed me vulnerable and allocated me a social worker.

Eventually, she bought me a tent, sleeping bag, pillow, and a weekend stay in Crystal Palace Park. People paid to go camping there, so she advised me not to say I was homeless. Instead, I should say I was having a weekend camping experience. It was the middle of summer, so after staying there one night and sitting in the hot tent doing nothing the next day, I decided this wasn't for me and left.

I struggled for a while being homeless and was all over the place, staying wherever - with Mum or Damon, sometimes. Eventually, my social worker got me into a hostel in Vauxhall called Centrepoint. It was supported accommodation for twenty-one males and seven females; finally, somewhere to rest my head. They took a little money from our benefits and provided breakfast and dinner.

Watching TV one day, I was surprised to see my friend, green-eyed Anthony, in the Sugababes' music video 'Push The Button.' He's the black guy dancing. Over the years, he eventually became a successful dancer, appearing on the X-Factor and dancing for artists such as Mariah Carey. It was another reminder of how I had messed up my potential through drug abuse.

Turning nineteen, I became good friends with a few housemates. Centrepoint also had a connection with a local drama group called Streets Alive. I'd always loved performing arts, so I joined immediately, attending four days a week for three hours a day. They paid us ten pounds after every session, a huge incentive. I drastically cut down on smoking white since this kept me busy doing something I enjoyed. A few weed-smoking friends from the hostel attended also, and we'd all buy skunk weed afterwards, then session all night. I fancied the pants off the teacher, a ginger woman named Emily, with whom I was utterly besotted.

I became good friends with an American guy from my hostel, Wolf, who grew up in New York as part of the Wolf set gang. He sold weed, which I sometimes sold for him, earning a few spliffs for myself.

Over the past few years, I'd developed a groin hernia, which had become a slight bulge. If I blew my nose or squeezed too hard when doing number two's, I sometimes felt the pressure push it out slightly. It wasn't a massive concern, as the doctor stated if it didn't majorly affect me, I could live with it. Still, I could have surgery if it caused problems.

I utilized the support from the hostel to get all the necessary requirements up and running, such as welfare benefits and a local doctor. After paying bills, I was left with roughly two hundred pounds a month; on these days, I usually bought white.

One payday, I smoked weed and white as usual and again turned into Whispers. The exact feeling again, and I became more accustomed to it every time like I was learning to control my superpower. That time I remember thinking I could jump out of my third-floor window and be OK; luckily, I didn't. I walked out into the Vauxhall bus garage in a t-shirt and boxers, with the school kids staring and laughing. Thankfully, some staff and residents guided me back, and an ambulance was called. I was checked over, and all was fine; I left the hospital and returned home feeling embarrassed. Still, I believed in my actions in the actual moment.

In my routine of drama class and smoking weed, my obsession with Emily, the teacher, kept me going. My yearning for fantasy and fulfilment was fed by any crumbs from her emotional table. A prolonged gaze into each other's eyes or her smile from my jokes. I assumed that intimate connection must be partially mutual from the emotions vibrating through me. How could I have had these emotions inside me without her feeling somewhat of the same? We were both human beings; she must have felt it to some degree.

We created a play together and performed it at local hostels and day centres; I was the protagonist. We always got positive feedback. After one performance, my fellow student handed me a piece of paper with a phone number. 'Oi Duppy, my sister Kirsty asked me to give this to you. I think she likes you.'

'Thanks,' I said, trying to remember her sister's appearance as she'd already left.

I soon got talking to Kirsty, and we clicked right away. She lived in Kingston, I'd visit her, and we quickly became a couple. She had a full-time job and treated me to gifts, including all-black Converse Allstars. She lived at home with her lovely parents; her bedroom was a loft conversion. This created specific problems at night because any 'jumping' on the bed could be heard downstairs. I thought, you must've heard the noise last night when speaking to her parents.

I soon attended a music course provided by The Prince's Trust. Twenty young adults learning various music knowledge for one week in the countryside, to perform for our family and friends at the end. On the third day, an attendee discovered the retreat's bar was left open. Some were scared, but seven of us drank all night.

One girl noticed the cash register contained around two hundred pounds and suggested taking it. I knew it was a terrible idea, so I dissuaded them, to no avail. I thought, she's taking it anyway; I might as well have a share, seventy pounds each. The next day, the staff notified us that we'd all be going home if the money wasn't returned.

No one confessed, angering those not involved for being punished for others' wrongdoing. We were given a few hours' deadline, saying we could all complete the course upon its return. I spoke with the others involved, but the girl said, 'I don't care; I'm keeping mine.' I put my cut in the bathroom and notified the staff that I'd found it there. They soon told us that £140 had been recovered and the course would continue.

That evening, they told me, 'We have information that you were involved, so you must leave tomorrow.'

'I only found it. That's not fair. The instigator hasn't even returned their share, yet they get to continue the course. If I'd taken it, I should've kept it as they did.' Another boy and I left the next day. That girl kept the money and continued the week. Life can sometimes be unfair, but it was my fault for being unwise.

18

Robberies, Hustling, and Heroin

L ife was great, but I also suffered what I now realise was depression. My room became very messy for a long time, which was a reflection of my mental state. There were many people in the hostel with various mental issues.

One resident friend must not have brushed his teeth for years because he had a thick layer of creamy yellow plaque on his top row. We all joked about it, always passing him the spliff last. It baffled me: why didn't he brush them? If he did just once, it'd be eradicated. But someone could've said the same about me; why doesn't he just clean his room? So I understand things aren't always as simple as they seem. He also built up like two hundred houseflies in his bedroom; we called it 'fly city.' We'd nudge his curtain, and thirty flies would fly around before returning to their spots.

Psychological depression and its effects are severe indeed. Mine stemmed from being an adult and not understanding my place in this world. I was confused about who I was and what I wanted to be. I'd repeat, 'Now, I'm going to live my life as the real me,' hoping that decision would somehow fix my problems. All I wanted was to be the best, most authentic version of myself. It fixed nothing!

Over time, I've learned that we must actively create who we are through action. Every moment we're alive is a chance to be whom we sincerely desire. Making a decision without a unified effort won't help because it's the action that makes things real.

Damon kept all our thousands of childhood photographs in a bag under his sink. One day when asking about them, he said they were all water damaged, so he'd thrown them away. This was heartbreaking; every picture we'd ever taken was gone forever.

My drama class had great connections. We were given two days to record a song in a professional E-M-I studio in Camden's Roundhouse Theatre. I sampled some church music, sped it up, and added a beat to it on 'FruityLoops,' that I'd downloaded to my hostel's tenant computer.

We had two days at the studio, and my depression was overpowering me on the first day, so I didn't attend. My friend Raz rang me, 'Duppy, where the fuck was you?'

'Ah, man, I was busy. Was it any good?'

'Bro, it was sick. You would've loved it, proper studio 'ting.' Today was made for you. Make sure you come tomorrow.'

'Yeah, you know what, I'll definitely come.'

The next day, I attended. Oh, my goodness, a twenty-four-year-old worker at the Roundhouse called Rosy was the most beautiful girl I'd ever seen, and she sat next to me. I wanted to marry her; I was delighted I had turned up. We were given a little tour and eventually entered the studio. A fantastic, real studio with professional equipment.

We all had about half an hour allocated each. I got Raz to drop a verse as I'd only written one and the chorus the night before. The engineer worked his magic, and the song was incredible. He gave me a copy, which I took home and impressed my friends. I eventually gave Damon my copy and asked him to send it to Uncle Gammospeng to help promote it.

A guy named Blaze had recently left prison and moved into my hostel. He was twenty-three, streetwise, and we clicked immediately. He smoked white and took me out to earn money with him. He was a ruthless street robber; I never enjoyed it. Still, through friendship, loyalty, and maybe slight intimidation, I went with him anyway.

We travelled all over his stomping ground, southeast London, robbing people for money and mobile phones. He'd lure people in by asking if they smoked weed, take them somewhere secluded on the promise of a free sample, and then ask them to put his number in their phones. But, of course, they weren't getting their phone back once it was in his hand. 'This is my phone now. Can I have this?' he'd say as if to cover his back by asking because, technically, it wasn't a robbery but a gift. 'We can fight for it right now if you want,' he regularly said.

He'd been to prison multiple times, so he knew the law. He tried to stay one step ahead by ensuring no CCTV was present, left no forensics, and we vacated immediately. We did two in a day if the prize wasn't enough. We must've robbed roughly thirty people during our time together; I felt sorry for them.

We'd score on Brixton frontline from a dealer named Bighead and then smoke in the Somerleyton flats down Coldharbour Lane. We did crazy things like smoke in phone boxes and random doorways. He smoked with prostitutes for blowjobs, but I didn't, as I was a romantic. I also met his friend Kitten, a street legend from the Brixton gang Twenty-Eights. We robbed for months until Blaze got re-imprisoned. You can only do so much crime before it catches up with you.

I soon started hanging with the other new smokers in my hostel as people regularly moved in and out. We went to Soho and sold people paracetamol, pretending it was whatever drug they wanted, whether coke, ketamine, or MDMA. They sometimes returned, saying it was good, and bought more, while others complained. But we diverted immediately, scored our drugs, and returned home happy. Many were doing similar things. Our resident friend named Scouse's favourite thing was knocking people out. Drugs became my priority, so I soon split from Kirsty.

A Peckham boy named Sean started selling crack within the hostel. His deals were tiny, and he was a slight bully. One night I borrowed his oyster card, 'Make sure you bring it back before 9am tomorrow.'

I got arrested the first time I returned with it late, but I had no excuse the second time. I entered Sean's room at about 9:45am; he left, returning with a hardened-knuckled glove on. WACK! 'Ahh, sorry, bro.' WHACK! He punched me twice, causing a lump on my head.

'Next time I tell you something, make sure you do it.' I was upset but understood the reality of keeping my word.

A friend from the hostel moved into his own flat in Camberwell, which became our new hangout. I met a pretty, petite light-skinned girl named Shortie at a party, and we soon became a couple. I was overwhelmed that I'd bagged a stunning girl.

My twentieth birthday soon approached, and I arranged a party at Mum's new flat in Thornton Heath. The day before, I chatted up a girl named Roxanne in Brixton. A good few of us turned up, and so did Roxanne. Shorty came too, so I kept the other girl hush-hush. Roxy started smoking skunk spliffs, but they had a weird potent smell. I asked her what it was and she went quiet. I discovered she was mixing heroin with weed. Mum soon got some crack too, and a few of us went into her bedroom to smoke. The non-crack smokers soon noticed the party had gone sideways, so most left. It was just me, Mark, and Roxanne.

Mark always got the girls and tried his luck with Roxy, but she liked me. He was persistent but clocked his efforts were in vain, so he left. We got busy, and the next day, she made more spliffs, and I asked to try them. 'No, I'm not giving you any; heroin is terrible addictive stuff,' she dissuaded me. Eventually, I had a few puffs. It buzzed me, and I threw up. We spent half the day chilling; each time she gave me a few tokes on her spliffs, it relaxed me.

I never realized its severity then, but I'd tasted heroin, a most insidious drug. This was the last piece of the puzzle that controlled my life for the next twelve years. After that, whenever I smoked crack with friends who smoked heroin, I took a few lines on the foil to bring me down. It was potent and speedily made us 'gouch,' basically falling asleep. Many warned me of its destructiveness and how you get sick without it, but I never got ill. Or so I thought. Because I never knew the symptoms, I didn't notice them immediately, but I soon felt weak, like I had a cold when without it.

After a month or so, it became an everyday addiction. Life revolved around sourcing it. To get well, you didn't need much. Because others in the hostel also took it, we supported each other and always had some on hand. It had various names, such as gear, dark, or brown, but we never called it heroin.

A friend gifted me an eighth ounce of crack to sell to make some money. I shared some with my friends and asked them to pay me a little something on their giro day. About two days later, I entered a friend's room full of people and smoked a dark pipe. BANG! I got punched from behind. It was Sean, with his two friends. 'Trying to sell white on my patch. Are you stupid?' Bang, Bang. He punched me some more.

'No, bro, sorry, I only shared it with them. They never gave me money.'

'Oi Axe, bang this youth for me.' His friend punched me. My supposed mate, Will, at whose birthday party I met Shorty, even supported them.

'Who owes Duppy money?' Sean asked. 'None of you owe him money anymore.' I could see my so-called friends were happy to not pay me. 'Where's the rest of it?'

'It's all gone, I swear.'

'If I go to your room and find it, I'm gonna fuck you up properly.' I had about fifteen stones left but hoped that where I'd hidden it, he wouldn't find it.

We entered my room and thank goodness it was a tip; clothes and stuff were everywhere. Sean searched around, looking in obvious places. I helped him, trying to keep him distracted. Finally, after ten minutes, he gave up. 'If you sell around here again, you'll get beaten worse.'

'I won't, I promise. I'm not that stupid.' It was hidden in a sock under a mountain of clothes. Phew, that was close. When my so-called friends who snaked me asked if I had any left, I said no, with a gleam in my eye, thinking, fuck you, cheeky bastards.

19

No Longer a Teenager

Young Jeezy was the hottest rapper, and we'd listen to him and Common. One day I asked Damon what Uncle Gammospeng thought of my song. He replied that he hadn't sent it correctly and would try to find the CD and send it again. But this never materialized, so that was another potential shot at my music career that ended prematurely.

My friend Smokey soon started selling Sean's crack in Soho. He got ten stones to bring back eighty pounds. He couldn't do deals like the other dealers who did three for twenty-five pounds, so he worked just to line Sean's pockets, barely scraping even.

Even after all the trouble with Sean, I gave in to temptation, taking five stones from him to sell. I had to bring him back forty pounds, so I had to work hard to earn one tiny ten-pound rock. I sold them ok twice, but the third time I messed up. I smoked a few, intending to make money back somehow I didn't, so I left my hostel, unsure of what to do. I made excuses when he phoned, eventually not answering.

My good friend, Richie, called saying he had some gear that evening, so I met him in the flats on Battersea Park Road. He was in the stairwell a few floors up, where we usually smoked. I smoked a pipe, and then three boys came up the stairs. It was Sean! He punched me with his reinforced glove and knocked me out cold. I recall feeling my head stamped upon and bouncing off the concrete staircase.

I awoke to just my friend standing there, so I ran away fast in a daze. Blood leaked from a large gash on my head, so I called an ambulance. They took me to the hospital; I got seven stitches in two wounds on the back of my head. Bandaged, I returned home to the staff, asking what'd happened. 'I had a fight with a stranger; I'll be fine, thanks.'

Richie later told me Sean forced him to set me up after giving him a free rock. Snitching would've made things worse; it's something I've never done and don't really agree with. When Damon found out, he wanted retribution, but involving him could've escalated the problems. I tried to stay away from Sean after that. Thankfully, Damon helped me to pay him, as he was pretty nasty, worshipping money. We made peace a week later, but I never truly forgave him for all the hurt he had caused me. I understand these were graves I dug myself, but his punishment was too severe.

On the 11th of March 2008, I scored with Smokey and Scouse and was about to smoke when a man in Vauxhall Gardens asked if I could source sixty-pound gear. The dealer did deals, so I'd gain three stones for getting it. I rang the dealer, who soon turned up. The runner was very paranoid about selling to strangers. I asked the man for the money, but he didn't trust me, saying, 'Only I'm doing the deal.' He was ten meters away from the dealer, who said she ain't serving someone she never knew. I tried to get it sorted for ten minutes, even offering the guy my shoes to hold. They eventually both walked off.

This angered me because I'd missed out on three stones and the initial smoke we scored. So I ran up to him, 'Oi bruv, do you know how much you made me lose? You better give me twenty pounds now.'

'No way. Piss off.' I head-locked him and then shouted to my friends who weren't far. They soon joined me, emptying the man's pockets. I got his phone, while Scouse got his I-Pod. As we walked off, a passer-by said, 'What are you doing? That's wrong.'

'He robbed me,' I replied.

I ran into a shop, hiding the phone underneath some beers. I stayed there, hoping no one saw me. Police soon turned up and took me outside, where the victim pointed me out. 'I didn't do anything; he robbed me, I stated. They searched me and found nothing. Handcuffed and intimidated, I said, 'I'll do the right thing; his phone is under there.'

'Right. You're under arrest on suspicion of robbery.'

'What do you mean? I was honest and gave back his phone.'

Afterwards, I realized that if I'd kept quiet, they wouldn't have found his phone and would've let me go. The police station's duty solicitor said I could get two to four years in prison for this. I was shocked as I never hurt him and felt it was a simple misunderstanding. I got bail and discovered the witness was an off-duty police officer. No wonder they turned up so quick.

One night I bumped into Mutya Buena from the Sugababes; my friend knew and spoke with her. I then met a girl named Corina through her boyfriend Ashman, with whom I'd recently become acquainted. He soon got imprisoned for eighteen months for a street robbery. It wasn't long before Corina confessed that she fancied me. I first considered it another man's territory, but we soon became a couple. She was twenty-seven, smoked white, and I enjoyed having an older missus.

There were many gay clubs in Vauxhall, and we all sold the clubbers paracetamol, making a killing every weekend. Then, one day, I scored from a dealer, and Tony, Anthony's cousin, turned up. 'Duppy, is it you?'

'Yes.'

'Duppy man, what are you doing smoking food? I shouldn't even serve you.'

'Come on, please, I need it.' I felt ashamed about buying hard drugs from a friend, but I needed my fix.

I bumped into Rastaman Janx in Kennington one day. He now smoked crack and had lost weight - how the tables turn. I never attended court for my robbery charge, but I thought nothing of it. Corina said I'd be going to jail, but I hardly did anything wrong in my eyes, so I brushed it off.

Having to source money every day, a friend introduced me to shoplifting. I wasn't great at it, but local corner shops started asking me to get chocolates, which I sold for fifty pence each. So I'd go to big supermarkets and steal about fifty bars to earn twenty-five pounds to get my two browns and one white.

On the 26th of August, my mum's birthday, I came through Victoria train station. Police checked everyone's tickets and caught me trying to slip through. Upon a namecheck, they said I had a warrant and arrested me. At the police station, they stated I wouldn't be getting bail as it was a severe offence, and I'd already skipped once. I spent two days in the station, getting very sick without gear. I experienced hot and cold sweats and couldn't sleep; it was hell, with microwaved dinners that tasted awful. The doctor gave me dihydrocodeine and sleeping tablets which only helped slightly. Finally, I was remanded, which meant I'd be imprisoned.

20

Off To Prison

The Feltham Youth Offenders Institute was where I went as I was twenty. I was glad to get there because I was starving for better food. They also gave me methadone, a medical heroin substitute, making me feel better. I was put on Albatross, the detox wing. Every wing is named after a bird, as the prison is designed in the shape of one. There were only six inmates on the whole wing, which could house around forty.

I was glad to smoke a roll-up, as the jail provided a smoker's pack on arrival. But on the detox wing, they kept our tobacco, only allowing three fags a day at breakfast, lunch, and dinner. My new surroundings were roughly six foot by ten, a bed with a thin blue mattress, a TV with five channels, and a toilet.

The next day the other inmates friendly interrogated me. 'What you in for, bruv?'

'Robbery. My solicitor said I should get a DRR; I'll be out soon.'

'Nah, mate, it takes forever; you're gonna be here months.'

'Your joking! That's long. I'm back in court in three weeks. Hopefully, I'll get out then.' They laughed.

We were allowed out for around two hours a day. Once in the morning, once in the afternoon, and half an hour for dinner. We had a pool table, table tennis, and a garden where we smoked.

My case got adjourned for three weeks at court for a pre-sentence report: a summary giving the judge all the facts. They still hadn't done it at my next appearance, so another adjournment. Fed up with the three fags a day, I detoxed off the methadone to go to a regular wing, eventually transferring to Partridge.

My Vauxhall Primary school friend, Pee-Wee, was there and had just begun an eighteen-year sentence for converting starter pistols into firearms. Feltham was filled with egotistical youngsters always fighting. On a regular day, the alarm bell sounded roughly fifty times. Once there were two fights on my wing simultaneously. The officers ran to stop one, while I witnessed another in the showers thirty seconds later.

My twenty-first birthday soon came, and I got shipped to an adult prison the next day: Wormwood Scrubbs. Six from Feltham went on the prison bus, and they put us in a six-man dorm for the first few nights. We were then housed on a regular wing. These wings were enormous, with four floors housing around two-hundred prisoners each. Time here was more challenging. The cells were Victorian, and the metal beds had considerable dips in the middle, giving us backaches.

Without a job or education, we only got out for half an hour a day, sometimes every other, and we had to shower and everything else within that time. Some veteran prisoners stated they loved it here, as they could easily acquire contraband. I once saw a parcel that was thrown over the wall land in the exercise yard. I'm sure the young officer saw, but it was wiser to turn a blind eye. For a newbie like me, time dragged exceptionally slowly. Finally, after two weeks, I was back in court and discovered that I was going to HMP Brixton. This was because you go to local prison allocated to each individual court.

It took hours to get checked in through reception and into a cell on G-wing, the detox wing. This cell was like a dungeon, which I shared with a random stranger. The prison was rough, with regular fights. I saw a guy get hit with a tuna can in a sock, which burst his eye socket open. I knew a few faces as there were many local Brixtonians here.

On the 15th of January 2009, I was back in court. After five months, I was released on a DRR, a drug rehabilitation requirement. This meant I had to go straight to rehab for three months. I never wanted to. I desired drugs but didn't care, as I wanted out of prison. I was released under strict conditions to attend probation the next day to be transported to a rehab facility in Southampton. I returned to Corina's, smoked, packed some bags, and turned up the next day. They instructed me on what the rehab would entail. Someone escorted me onto the train with a contact number and directions.

Upon arrival, I was greeted by friendly staff who took me through the ins and outs, rules, etc. The rehab residents had been there for varying times, some a few days while others for months. I shared a room with Marcel, an older street legend from Bournemouth. He told me stories of how he'd slept with roughly five hundred women and would be in a club and see an average of three women he'd done it with. 'Sweet Dreams' by Beyonce was the latest song, and it was nice being out of prison.

We'd spend most of the day in groups discussing ways to conquer addiction and attend Narcotics Anonymous meetings some evenings. But the staff soon realised I came here just to get out of jail because I repeated that I'd use drugs at the first opportunity. This became a problem, as the other residents were seriously seeking sobriety. So after about twenty days, they said I could leave if I wanted. If I'd known this earlier, I would've left immediately. So, three weeks in, they contacted my probation officer, stating it wasn't working out and I should continue my DRR in the community. Finally, I could soon smoke again. I packed, said my goodbyes, and got the train back to London.

Upon my return, I scored drugs immediately. I was instructed to contact probation to sort out my DRR and change it into a community-based one. This went pear-shaped. I never followed up with my appointments and returned to my old ways. I knew I'd have another warrant out but didn't care as I lived for the moment, only worrying about my next smoke. I soon needed heroin again every day to function.

Damon worked in Ted Baker as a sales assistant around that time. He mentioned that his colleague Vanessa White had joined a group of female singers, and they'd soon release music. She eventually became a worldwide superstar as a part of The Saturdays.

Corina had lost her flat, so we stayed at an alcoholic's house in Myatts Field Brixton. He claimed he hadn't washed for five years. He'd wet himself, fall asleep, and continue wearing the same clothes for weeks. I never really knew how to make money, so I depended on Corina a little, but we always found a way. Unfortunately, I went downhill, and she lost respect for me. I was not the man she met, as heroin controlled my life, and I wasn't a fantastic provider. She spent more time away, becoming very close to her friend Manic. We eventually split, as she stated she needed a real man who could provide, and I could barely support myself.

I was homeless again and only concerned about drugs. However, we were still close, and when Manic went to jail, Corina let me stay with her at his flat in West Norwood. This was when Blaze, my street-robbing old bestie, returned from prison. He visited me right away and was hench. I introduced him to Corina, and they liked each other. He was definitely a provider, so it was a correct match. It never bothered me, as drugs were my priority, and I had a lot of love for them both.

I soon saw two songs on TV called 'Skinny Jeans' and 'Pack Up' by Eliza Doolittle. Wow, my college friend who attended my seventeenth birthday party was storming the charts. I was starstruck that my old mate had made it, but this proved how much I was wasting my life. She had two UK top tens, and her attending my party was my little claim to fame.

I stayed here and there, shoplifting and hustling every day. I had shops all over south London that bought various items from me, such as tuna, cheese, meat, washing up gels, chocolates and sweets. So, I terrorised every local shop stealing whatever I could. I didn't have many places to bathe, so I smelled - slightly. I sometimes got caught by security, and if I'd already been banned from their shop, they'd call the police. When they arrived, it was game over; I'd be returning to prison.

Once those handcuffs got put on, there was no more freedom until the system decided on it. So, I was back in the cells, on the blue mattress, clucking for gear, reading the writing on the ceiling: Sick and tired of feeling sick and tired? Call Crimestoppers Anonymously.

Time went so slowly; sometimes, I'd be in the police station for multiple days before getting to prison. I felt like Kunta Kinte from *Roots* on the slave ship, with no control over my reality. The police station is like hell when addicted to heroin.

In court, my sentence was revoked. They re-sentenced me to thirty months, reduced to twenty for my early guilty plea, which gets you one-third off. Luckily, we serve half in jail with shorter UK prison sentences and the other half free on licence. So, I'd do ten months, with five taken off for what I had previously served.

I landed in HMP Brixton and went straight to G-Wing, which had all new faces. I settled back in, struggling to survive without money, but I had a kind cellmate who shared with me. I was a small fish, scraping by, but luckily got Mum's or Damon's odd postal order of ten to twenty pounds to keep me going. One day I noticed the most beautiful woman I'd ever seen. Her name was Miss Dyer; people said she was the footballer Kieron Dyer's cousin. She looked super-hot in her prison officer uniform.

I was rapping in a cell one day with a few others when I heard a familiar voice. It was R.A, my favourite rapper from the Roadside Geez. I was gassed and asked him what he was in for. 'Ah, some m-charge thing, but hopefully, I'm gonna buss case.' M-charge was prison slang for murder.

I soon learned I was classified as a D-cat, not knowing what it meant. I asked a fellow inmate, 'Ya bomboclat, you're lucky, D-cat, your nice bruv. Get transferred immediately; it's live. Drugs galore, phones, out all day, everything.'

'Sounds good. I'm gonna get onto the guvs and try to sort that out asap.' I discovered the D-cat Brixton transferred to was Stanford Hill, but they only accepted prisoners on 20ml methadone or less. So, I cut down as fast as possible; a month later, I was on the bus off to D-cat.

It was a three-hour ride to the Isle of Sheppey, which contained three prisons: a B-cat, HMP Swaleside housing prisoners serving five years plus, HMP Elmley, a C-cat, and my new home, HMP Stanford Hill. Upon arrival, the officer stated, 'There aren't high fences here; if you run, we won't chase ya.' They let us off the bus without handcuffs, and this seemed more like a holiday camp than a prison.

All single cell's this time. There were no locks on the doors, as the toilets were located on the landing. We were allowed out of our cells from 9am until 10:30pm to enjoy the swimming pool, gym, table tennis, snooker, etc. We even had a vast grass area to sunbathe. The first night there, we newbies from Brixton managed to get five pounds of hash weed, the same size I'd get on the streets. This jail was sweet indeed.

I made a few friends, started an education course, and got a job that paid excellent wages of fifteen pounds a week for twenty minutes of cleaning each morning. But because we were out all day, time ticked slowly. One day felt as long as three days in a regular prison.

I also fancied the math teacher. She was old and not that pretty, but authoritative figures did something for me, especially in uniform. Whether it's policewomen, prison officers, nurses, or teachers, I get a crazy attraction for that forbidden fruit.

We were regularly piss tested for drugs, so we drank multiple litres of water to dilute our pee when our test slip came through. They even had dilution tests to see how watered down it was. I soon knew the bigger fishes, and because I had only three months left, they paid me for errands they couldn't afford to get caught for. Such as delivering four big bottles of vodka to house block B. Or pressing the fire alarms at night. I did this so they could collect drugs from prisoners on other spurs, as we all assembled in the same area.

After doing it three times, I got called into the governor's office. 'We have information that you pressed the fire alarm two days ago.'

'It wasn't me. Whoever said that is probably trying to divert the attention off themselves. There aren't even cameras there to prove my innocence.' I replied flamboyantly.

'We believe it's you, and that's that. You've been reclassified as a C-cat, so you'll leave tomorrow.' And just like that, my time in D-cat was over. I was transferred to Elmley, where I spent one night before returning to Scrubs for local release. I was back in a shithole, where time dragged. But luckily, I only had a month left.

21

Thornton Heath

Prison release day is always great; it feels like a birthday. I got my forty-seven pounds discharge grant and scored straight away. But unfortunately, I was still homeless, so I stayed with Mum. I returned to my old ways, smoking every day and shoplifting. I also stood outside the train station, asking people for their old travel cards, then resold them. This earned me roughly fifteen pounds an hour and became my safer source of drug money. I spotted Ashman, Corina's ex-boyfriend, on the TV show *Gordon Behind Bars*, where chef Gordon Ramsey had set up a food business in HMP Brixton. I was glad to be free.

It was summer, and I soon befriended all the local young gees who, like in Brixton, enjoyed having somewhere to smoke their weed. An older G named Fester ran the area, and I'd buy gear from him regularly. Above Mum lived an American man named Mark, MD, short for Mad Dog. He was from New York, one month older than Mum; he had killed someone in self-defence, getting five years for manslaughter. He was then sent back to his birthplace, England. He was a martial arts fanatic and became my sensei and one of my best friends. He told me a story of a fight he had when he was sixteen. His larger opponent had body-slammed him onto his head, so MD finger-jabbed him in his eye. His eye fell out, hanging on what looked like a bit of snot.

I also met a sixteen-year-old boy named Josh, a prolific criminal. He introduced me to pulling on car door handles. We'd go around, preferably at night, pulling car doors and entering any unlocked ones. We'd take any valuables, mostly Tom-Tom's. Josh drove, so he'd take the car if they left a spare key. Once, we got an Audi A6. When I was away, Josh bumped into my good older friend I'd recently met named Buds, who took the keys and control of the car. They sold it to Fester for one hundred pounds, and I never saw a penny.

I bumped into Corina one day, who told me that Janx was in prison for murder. With how gangster he was, I can't say I was surprised. Back in the day, he regularly hollered, 'Me kill people,' and spoke of events back in Trinidad.

Next door to Mum lived a crack smoker named Trish. She was forty-two and had mental health issues. Being homeless, sleeping in Mum's garden shed half of the time because Steff didn't want me around, I decided to sleep with Trish a few times for somewhere to stay. She wasn't ugly, the sex was ok, and I needed shelter; so I did the necessary, humouring the young gees.

One day Mum's Jamaican friend fell asleep at her house with his expensive gold chain on. 'Oi Dups, we can get like five hundred pounds for that; come we take it,' Josh said.

'No way, we can't do that. He's a nice guy.' Mum was also against the idea. After some persuasion, Josh eventually got some scissors and spent twenty minutes cutting it off. 'Yes, I've got it. Let me and my pal go to Bromley to sell this. I've got a guy who gives top dollar.'

'No way, I'm coming with you, I said.'

'This is my house; I'll have to deal with him when he wakes up. Make sure you bring me some money back,' Mum said.

Josh, his friend, and I travel to Bromley. 'Wait here; the shopman will be funny if he sees too many people,' Josh stated. He soon returned. 'I got £120 for it. Forty pounds each.'

'Are you joking? No way he gave £120.'

'I think he knew it was stolen. That's all he gave,' Josh reiterated. He left with his mate, with his body language blatantly showing he was lying.

I returned to the shop. 'My friend just sold my gold chain here. He said he got £120; is that correct?'

'No, fella, let's just say I gave him at least double that,' the shopkeeper replied. I was sickened that my friend could betray me, knowing the problems my mum would face. Mum soon rang. 'Dan, he's woken up and is going berserk. That was a gift from his daughter and had a lot of sentimental value. He's fuming; he's bringing people to smash Josh's head in.'

I never knew what to do, so I did what'd take the stress away; scored. I intended to save Mum some but ended up smoking it all, returning with only ten pounds. I felt terrible because poor Mum dealt with all the drama while we were out. I got Mum a ten-pound stone but felt incredibly guilty.

Damon and his girlfriend Danielle lived about ten minutes away and sometimes visited. In April, we saw my school friend Aggro Santos' latest song on TV, 'Candy', featuring the Pussycat Doll Kimberly Wyatt. Wow, this was incredible, but it highlighted where I should be. I should be on TV, not sick, waiting on drug dealers.

One night I was selling a Tom-Tom to the chicken shop with Josh when police stopped and searched us. 'I broke my knee six weeks ago, so I'm putting you in cuffs as I don't fancy chasing you. You're druggie scum, so you're definitely getting nicked tonight for something.' When the other officer questioned the shopkeeper, I ran, still wearing cuffs.

I was getting away but took the wrong turn up a dead end, and he caught me halfway over a fence. I kicked back, thinking it was unwise, hitting him slightly. He got mad and shoved my face on the floor. I couldn't breathe, but he didn't care. 'Stop resisting,' he shouted while pushing his finger into the pressure point behind my ear as I lay totally still. I was caught, there was no point in resisting, yet he continued to take his anger out on me.

I was charged with theft from a motor vehicle and returned to prison. In HMP Brixton, I shared a cell with a street legend from East London named Byfield; almost everyone feared him. He told me about his notorious father Chopper. He hustled and taught me how to make fake heroin by crushing and burning paracetamol. He sold some but went to court and never returned. I was left with the phoney gear and stress I never needed. So I gave it away, as people complained it was rubbish.

I also met another street legend named, Azwad, another Brixton twenty eight. He told me how he escaped from The Old Bailey court, which I googled many years later and verified.

On association one evening two weeks in, the officers shouted, "Grossett."

'Yes, guv.'

'Pack your stuff. You're going home.' I was given a fourteen-day sentence in my absence, so I'd already served my time. Great, I was free and, once again, went straight to score. I returned to my mum's house and my previous lifestyle. My father then gave me a small painting job in his flat and paid me cash daily.

One day on my way home, someone offered to sell me a travel card at Streatham Common train station. 'I'm OK, but can you score?' Gareth was his name; he scored and took me to his house. Vicky, his girlfriend, was there; we smoked. She flirted with me. 'I'm working again tomorrow. I'll come round and smoke with you if you want?'

The next day, the same thing happened. Then on the third day, when Gareth was out scoring, Vicky kissed me. I felt guilty because I'm not a homewrecker, but they constantly argued, and she was cute. She'd repeatedly pinch my bum as we walked down the street and played footsie under the table. 'I can see you blatantly flirting with Daniel, Vicky,' I heard Gareth say.

They had a huge argument two weeks in, and he slapped her, then jumped on the bus home. We got the next bus, and as we passed her stop, she never got off. 'I'm staying with you, Daniel.'

'He shouldn't have slapped you, but you should go home.'

'No, I ain't going back.' So, we went to my mum's and literally became a couple. Days later, she snuck home when Gareth was out to collect some belongings. We both used brown, so I also fed her habit.

Steff soon got me a job as a kitchen porter in the pub he worked at in Herne Hill. Cash in hand and a pizza to take home every night. Vicky started turning up and waiting for me to finish, so we could get well together, which looked unprofessional. Without a methadone prescription, we needed gear every day to function. It wasn't easy saving some for the next day. Sometimes I'd be working, feeling terrible, disguising my sneezes. But we'd score immediately with my wages each night.

One evening after scoring in Clapham Common, I bumped into Gareth. He and his mate took me to a bin shed. 'This is the guy who ran off with my girlfriend.'

'I'm sorry, G, it's not even like that.'

His friend slapped me, 'You're lucky you're twenty-three; otherwise, I'd cut ya.' My main thought was, please don't spot the four stones I've got in my mouth. They'd certainly take them if they knew.

They let me go, 'Tell Vicky to call me right away.'

'I definitely will, G.' I went home unscathed but had to watch my back.

Vicky spent that Christmas at Mum's with me, and I was working at the bar on New Year's Eve when I noticed her chatting with a man. When my shift finished, she was nowhere to be seen. Then, outside, I caught her kissing him. We argued, and she was obviously in the wrong. But when she started walking off, being wrapped around her little finger had me pleading with her to not leave me. Oh, what a sucker I was for females sometimes.

I soon managed to rent a room from Damon's landlord in Addiscombe. One night, I returned home from scoring, and after repeatedly knocking, I got no answer. Where was Vicky? I eventually climbed around the back and spotted her inside with a man. I shouted through the letterbox, but she seemed happy to leave me outside in the snow all night, so after repeatedly warning her, I called the police.

When they arrived, she opened the door, and even though it was my room and I paid the rent, they said I should get some things and leave as I couldn't prove it. So, I slept in some flats and returned the next day. We argued, and Vicky said she met a dealer with loads of crack, which he supposedly flushed when the police arrived. I knew they must've done stuff but sucker me forgave her.

A week later, I returned home and found a housemate's door was broken. His big flatscreen TV was gone, and Vicky was nowhere to be seen. Two days later, I discovered that she and Gareth had stolen it, and they were back together. So after roughly four months, Vicky and I were over. I got evicted by the landlord and was homeless again.

I soon got arrested for shoplifting, and after being taken to a police station in central London, I went to HMP Belmarsh.

On the first day, I spotted my old bestie, Aaron; he was in the cell next to me. I got twelve weeks in court, and upon returning to jail, I saw Tia Sharp's murderer Stuart Hazell in a holding cell. He looked at me, then looked down, shaking his head. It's crazy; the things people do for sick pleasure are abominable. I wonder how many people have thrown their lives away for quick sexual gratification.

I did my six of twelve weeks and returned to society. I was still homeless, but luckily Trish, Mum's neighbour, had a friend named Michael who got me a room in his shared accommodation in Croydon. It was a twelve-room dump, full of crackheads and alcoholics and ridden with bedbugs. But it was better than nowhere. My housemates soon became my new smoking buddies; it was a little community within itself. We all looked forward to each other's paydays as we usually shared drugs, but there were always arguments and shouting.

After spending two weeks in jail for shoplifting, I kept my methadone script instead of detoxing, as it would be a lifeline in the community. So at least I wasn't sick every day. This came at a good time because there was a drought for heroin in all of south London. No dealers had anything decent; you could literally smoke one hundred pounds worth and still feel sick. This continued for months.

I soon met a dealer, Wayne, who liked me, and I eventually started selling for him. He'd leave me with about three hundred pounds worth of gear, coming each night to collect the takings. He usually just sent the customers to my house, as it was a drug hotspot. This was tough for me as a smoker, and sometimes I'd nick some from the half-sixteenths and rewrap them, hoping the customers never noticed. I didn't take too much, though, as I knew there were limits to what I could conceal.

One night, there was a knock on the main door. It was a girl I knew named Star, so I let her in. I looked out my window and saw a man I'd seen before locally. I felt uneasy and paranoid from smoking, so my friend Reds and I started pushing my fridge up against my door. Boom, boom, boom! Two masked men kicked it and burst in, waving knives around. 'Gimme the drugs and money,' they shouted. I threw the four browns I had left onto the bed and told them Wayne had already collected the cash. They grabbed the stones and left. Reds cheekily laughed about it afterwards but soon noticed they'd taken his phone; that took the smile off his face.

After around two months, the dealing became more of a headache than it was worth, so I stopped, as I was only getting paid twenty-five pounds a day. I could make more money doing a new crime someone had shown me: stealing lead off roofs. I'd go around at night looking for easy targets, then climb up and rip it off. A local scrapyard didn't require ID, so I cashed in my metal every morning. Within a few months, I'd taken almost every accessible bit of lead in main Croydon. I even did the whole of Reds' estate, which housed thousands.

One morning, I was up four storeys on a roof, and the police came. I quickly climbed down, and there was a fence between an officer and me. 'Stay where you are. Do not move.' I paused for a second, ready to give up, then thought, what have I got to lose? So, I ran.

'Taser, taser, taser,' he shouted. I hopped many fences going through gardens. They even had the dogs out. Finally, I found a spot in a garage reasonably far from where I started and stood still for about an hour. When I came out, the police were gone. That was close.

I visited Mum's one night and surprisingly noticed a member of So Solid Crew in her room with her. I won't mention names because 'Dan man don't snitch,' but I was impressed that Mum still had her magic touch.

I found a way to climb up in Reds' estate to the main roof with huge lead panels. The first night I made £140. The second night, £125. The cab drivers charged me twenty pounds for the two-minute drive to the scrapyard; they knew I was doing something dodgy. Then on the third night, the residents must have heard me because amid taking the lead, a helicopter turned up. It shone its light on me, and I knew I stood little chance of escape. I ran to get down, but the police were there waiting.

Back to prison, it was: HMP Highdown. I pleaded guilty and got thirteen months. Arriving on the detox wing, I bumped into a familiar face; Josh. We were still mates, and it was nice having him watch my back. I settled in and noticed people walking around with atrocious haircuts. I thought there was no way I'd do a fade as bad as these, so I practised on Josh. My trim was the best on the wing. Before long, I cut hair regularly and was the go-to guy. This was great, as nothing is free in prison, so people paid me for my services, usually in drugs or food. I started hitting the gym three times a week and lived comfortably.

Whilst inside, Mark Duggan was shot and killed by the police, which caused riots all over the country. Croydon suffered some of the worst there was. Mum was in Mayday, Croydon's hospital, and said she left and nicked a bottle of water from a shop; bless her. There was a 140-year-old shop named Reeves Corner, which was burnt down. When they eventually sentenced the arsonist to eleven-and-a-half years in prison, I noticed he was the guy who robbed me at knifepoint when I was selling drugs. What a small world. After six and a half months, I left prison at over twelve stone - in the best shape of my life.

22

South Norwood/Selhurst

O n the first day out, as usual, I immediately scored. But unfortunately, I was still homeless, so I stayed with Mum for a few days before bumping into Michael, whom I lived with at the hostel. He was with Lana and a cute girl named Chloe. He had a flat in Beaulah Hill, so we all went there and smoked. We stayed there, and the next day Lana told me that Chloe fancied me.

I flirted with her for two days, then asked her out. She said yes. She also needed somewhere to stay as she was from Leicester, so Mike let us have his bedroom with him sleeping on the sofa. He didn't mind because I was a decent grafter, so I always had money and drugs. And as long as the narcotics kept coming, Mike was alright. He had mental health issues and got a lot of money from benefits, but he'd smoke his entire payment in one night; he was a proper crackhead.

Once, he walked down the street, and a teenager offered him white. 'Why are you offering me? I might not smoke that,' Mike said.

'Look at you; of course you take crack,' the kid replied. That made me laugh

I soon had a brown habit again, so I started shoplifting locally. I'd travel anywhere, and regularly the missions took hours. It wasn't easy; it was a real headache stealing every day. But I was OK if I made enough money to score Chloe came grafting sometimes, and she'd distract the staff while I loaded up Occasionally I'd sleep until the evening when most shops were closed. Then

I'd go grafting, hoping for a miracle. I'd mentally pray every time, wishing for an easy source of money, and nine out of ten times, I succeeded. I usually wouldn't enter the shop if I hadn't said my prayer. Worse case, I'd ask people for change to make ten pounds minimum to get my brown.

I'd walk the streets for hours, and one night I noticed an older people's home window was open, with a big flatscreen TV inside. I snuck through and found a bag containing a bank card and pin. I went straight to the cashpoint and withdrew the maximum; three hundred pounds. I felt guilty, but this was my drug-addicted reality.

Buds, a streetwise ex-gunman, became my best friend. He always positively guided me, uplifting me to be noble. Mum also loved him, and he called her Mummy Lu-Lu. Mum soon moved to South Norwood, and Chloe and I stayed with her sometimes. She had a significant health problem and took around ten pills every day. Being a friendly spirit, Mum brought two young guys home one evening. They were cool and spoke with Chloe and me more; she said one had a nice smile.

I was soon recalled back to prison for twenty-eight days for missing probation. An artificial cannabis substitute called 'spice' had flooded the prisons, which got you super high. I took three puffs on someone's spliff and was on another planet within minutes. A spice attack, it's called; I ran headfirst into the post box and started doing fireballs at the officers. They locked up the whole wing because of me. I was taken to healthcare but returned the next day to many shocked inmates who thought I was a goner.

I also saw an eighteen-stone gym obsessive named Gorilla have a fight with two roughly ten-stone youngsters. He got punched and shat himself. The whole wing laughed when the poo dropped out of his tracksuit bottoms onto the floor. While inside, Mum became unwell, and Chloe called an ambulance that saved her life. They said Mum might have died within hours had the call not been made; I thanked Chloe dearly.

I left Highdown after four weeks, with Chloe meeting me at the gate. We went home, smoked, and had sex. I then rushed to probation and rang her after.

'Daniel, I've left. I'm not at your Mum's anymore; I'm staying with a friend.'

'What do you mean? Aren't you still my girlfriend?'

'Erm, erm.' she hung up. I called back with no answer. I returned to find all Chloe's stuff was gone, and a note saying she was sorry, she loves me, but we're over. Within the next few days, I discovered she was with that same boy she said had a nice smile - the irony of it. I tried to win her back, but her heart was set elsewhere. So, I returned to what I knew; shoplifting and smoking.

Mum soon met a new fella, a Rastaman called Jah-Man. He was 6ft 3, a bit of a preacher, and believed that women should serve their man's every need. Mum had fallen pretty hard for him, and he basically moved in. He was slightly peculiar and never wanted me to stay over. I regularly slept in blocks of flats and started sleeping in MD's bin shed on Mayday road. Someone had left a double mattress inside, so I'd sleep on that and graft throughout the day. My life was a constant merry-go-round of drugs, crime, and prison.

I soon turned twenty-six and had nothing but the clothes on my back and the hope that one day things might improve. I was blessed to have Mum, though, who loved me with all her heart. We were like Bonnie and Clyde, and everyone whose path she crossed cherished her. Then, I met a girl in Croydon named Jasmine. I didn't fancy her, but she was kind and helped me with money sometimes. We became a couple, but I never enjoyed kissing her, especially in public. She and I viewed a flat she'd possibly move into, and I pointed out that half of the roof was made from lead.

A new Caucasian female rapper named Iggy Azalia stormed the music scene, highlighting the changing world. Life was hard; I'd wear the same clothes for days and sometimes thought the shop staff could smell that I was a thief. Once, I sat at the back of a bus when a young girl boarded. Upon coming upstairs, her face screwed up, with her hand covering her nose. My wet trainers and socks stank.

I was still getting arrested, but I was given chances with DRRs as shoplifting wasn't considered the most heinous crime. I'd usually breach these, so I did many short stints in prison here and there. I soon broke up with Jasmine, so I decided to give that flat we viewed a visit.

I put a green work visor on to look official and went through about five gardens to get to it. I'd yanked all the lead off the roof but soon noticed a helicopter above. I thought no way it was here for me, but it was. The police walked through the back gate and arrested me. A neighbour whose garden I scaled had called them. I might've succeeded if I'd only noticed the back gate initially.

Back to prison again. HMP Thameside this time, as I'd attended a different court because it was a Saturday. It was privately run by Serco and had a massive football pitch, computers, and showers in the cells; it was sweet. Back on a detox wing, back on methadone, starting from the bottom. But I had a skill, barbering. So, I promoted myself and started cutting hair upon acquiring some clippers. I bumped into Ashman for the first time since Vauxhall, but he hardly mentioned Corina.

While inside, Damon told me Mum was in the hospital but never declared much. Prisons were flooded with spice, so I smoked it regularly. My friend G arrived, so we shared a cell. I completed the Peace Education course, which taught prisoners worldwide that inner peace is imperative and can still be found in prison. It was created by Prem Rawat, who started preaching about peace at around age twelve. Then, after a few months, back to freedom, it was.

I visited Mum immediately to find her beaten and bruised with thirty-something stitches on her face. Her boyfriend Jah-Man had punched her during an argument. She showed me a picture of herself one week after it had happened. Her face had been beaten to a pulp, swollen to twice its normal size; I cried. Mum never pressed charges, so he was still a free man. Buds and I wanted to hurt him, but I knew we'd just get imprisoned, and I wanted my freedom to look out for Mum. When it eventually went to court, he got away with self-defence, even though my frail eight-stone, 5ft 8, unwell mother had hardly scratched him. What dimension was the CPS living in?

I soon got housed in a hostel in Sylvan Hill near Crystal Palace. As usual, I returned to crime and drugs. Reds' parents were wealthy and funded his drugs every day. He regularly manufactured stories to sponge money from them. He said he'd been arrested and needed to pay a fine one night. They were in their late sixties, yet they drove for over an hour at 1:00am to bring him thirty pounds. He got the cash and pointed them to a police officer when they arrived. 'I think your son has just had you over. He wasn't fined,' the officer told them. Reds and I quickly left.

He was a bit drunk and almost got into a fight. I ran, backed him up, and separated them. 'Where's the money? I can't find it. Duppy, man, I must've fucking dropped it,' Reds moaned. We retraced our tracks searching, but after twenty unsuccessful minutes, we headed home. We then bumped into my Rastaman drug dealer at West Croydon, so we briefly chatted.

'Are you ok, mate? Your friend just knocked you out,' a stranger said.

My face was hurting, and I could not remember anything. Reds groaned further down the road, 'Duppy, c'mon, let's go.' What on earth had just happened?

'I fucked up your friend. The boy just knocked you out,' my Rasta friend told me.

"Huh, why'd he do that? Are you sure? I can't remember anything."

'Yeah, man, the white boy over there, mi bust him up fi you. The youth is mad. Bloodclaat.' Supposedly, Reds had punched and knocked me out cold. It didn't make sense.

I joined Reds to find him in agonizing pain, and we started walking home. 'What happened?'

'Those guys just beat me up. My arm is hurting; I think it's broken.'

'Who knocked me out? They said you did it.'

'Duppy, I can't remember. I'm in pain; let's just go home.' So, we headed back to his flat and got our heads down.

The following day, he pulled out thirty pounds. 'Look what I found down my boxers.' After all that drama, he'd never lost the money; he was just too drunk to remember where he'd put it. He was a spoilt thirty-seven-year-old who leeched off his wealthy parents and admitted he'd ragefully punched me to take out his anger. When I next spoke with my Rasta friend, he told me that Reds punched me and then him, so he and his friend beat him up, breaking his arm in three places. I thought that was his karma for hitting me for no reason.

Mum eventually lost her flat, so she stayed with friends. She gave me our only remaining photo album to keep safe. But unfortunately, I soon got imprisoned again for shoplifting and lost my hostel. While serving various sentences, I completed courses such as art, cooking, health and safety, and peer mentoring.

Upon my release, the hostel gave me six months to collect my belongings. But feeding my addiction was my uneasy priority, so I didn't get them. This broke my heart because I'd lost our final remaining childhood pictures. But I tried to look on the bright side, thinking I've still got Mum. I cherished every moment as a person is worth much more than pictures.

Mum eventually moved into a lovely Selhurst flat opposite the Brit School that Amy Winehouse and Adele had once attended. Damon and Danielle started staying with her. I visited to discover they slept in Mum's double bed, with her sleeping on a blow-up mattress in the front room. 'Are you taking the piss, bro? How are you gonna make Mum, who's getting old and isn't well, sleep on a blow-up bed while you and your girlfriend take hers? Na bruv, that's wrong.' They soon switched back.

I got imprisoned in HMP Thameside again, and I did some research into Islam. It felt like the correct path, so I took my Shahada and officially became a Muslim. I also started conditioning my arms. I'd go to the exercise yard and repeatedly hit the metal pull-up bars with my forearms and palms. Eventually, I could hit it hard, and it felt soft like rubber. I also saw my old dealer Fester, who got fourteen years for selling guns to an undercover policeman.

I left prison this time on a different heroin substitute, Subutex. Every day, I went to the chemist and never worried about getting sick. There was a large shop two minutes from my chemist, and I shoplifted there roughly twice a week for months. I took almost every perfume on display until they eventually had only cheap ones that weren't worth taking. I always gave Mum gifts, and my household got first dibs on stolen goods.

While Damon stayed with Mum, he had a computer with internet access. He showed me many videos on YouTube, enlightening me about all the knowledge he'd learned over the years, like the Fibonacci sequence and sacred geometry. I also studied Mike Tyson, watching his early training and fights. Damon introduced me to 'The Secret' by Rhonda Byrne, which I highly recommend. It speaks about the law of attraction and how to attract what you want into your life. It says we can ask the universe for anything, and as long as we believe and put the effort in, there are no limits to what it can provide. The only limitation is our imagination or self-belief. Over time, I've found this to be true.

I read many books throughout my jail sentences. While on basic without a TV for a month, I read roughly half of the Holy Quran. I also read one on the whole of human history. I learned that human civilization has mostly just warred and killed each other for dominance since records began, which has only changed within the last few decades. I also read David Icke's *The Lion Sleeps No More*, *The Human Universe* by Brian Cox, *The Vision of Ramala*, *The Kabbalah*, and many others. This powerful knowledge moulded me into who I am today. Much of the knowledge I learned is emulated in this book. We aren't born wise; we gain wisdom from every interaction. Just as we attend gyms to increase our physical strength, mental strength is a crucial component of self-actualization.

I stayed at Mum's, and Damon being there brought a more normal feeling to the household. Also, being on Subutex, my life became relatively stable. I still shoplifted regularly, as I enjoyed using drugs and used them most days. But again, every local shop soon knew my face, so I travelled further to find ones to steal from.

23

Injecting/Portland Road

I was twenty-seven when I met a girl called Jamie one day; she was younger than me. She was a prostitute on gear, but she injected it. We were basically a couple but never kissed or slept together. A few weeks in, I was tempted to try a needle. Wow, I could instantly put into my body what I'd usually smoke in an hour, and the buzz was ten times stronger. I officially became an injector. I was at the lowest of the low in the drug game, something I never thought I'd be. I carried needles everywhere and found myself regularly in stairwells, toilets, or anywhere I could inject.

I was soon back in prison for commercial burglary and theft. But, upon landing in my local jail, HMP Highdown, I started cutting hair immediately and lived pretty well. I was no longer a little fish, that was for sure. I smoked spice almost every day inside, and everyone loved me as I cut all the mandem's hair. I did eight haircuts in one day once.

I loved attending the Muslim prayer service on Fridays; when free, I was too consumed by my addiction to go. I intended to sort my life out, most times in prison, so I usually detoxed off the medication. So, upon release, I no longer had a script; I went back to freedom and scoring immediately, as usual.

Mum had a new boyfriend, Brian, a drinker and supposed Freemason, but Damon never liked him. Mum had bought us a soundcard, an expensive microphone, and decent headphones one Christmas. We returned one evening to find the headphones with two precise scissor cuts straight through the wire.

Brian slyly said they must've got caught in a door or something, but we knew he did it. Another time Brian told Damon that he'd make a good Freemason, and Damon replied by punching his face.

Mum eventually moved again to Portland Road, South Norwood. I stayed with her as she never wanted me sleeping on the streets. We heard through the grapevine that Jah-Man was telling people he was going abroad to traffic drugs. Funnily, we next heard that he got caught at the airport and got over six years in prison. Yes, that's your karma and the prison sentence you deserved for hospitalizing Mum. It shows that if you tell even one person a secret, there's a possibility that they could divulge it. Whereas if you tell nobody, it can't be exposed.

Life was tough. Every day I needed heroin; otherwise, I'd be sick. So I had to find money out of thin air. I wouldn't say I liked grafting, but I loved it when I made money and had my drugs. Many local friends gave me lists of items to get for them, which I'd sell at half price or less.

I'd nick anything like alcohol, tools, curtains, and toys; if it was accessible, I'd get it. Sometimes, it was fun, the thrill of walking into shops and taking anything I wanted. I got away with it 95% of the time. If I did get caught, when lucky, I'd return the stuff and leave. I was constantly looking to earn, so I'd take any opportunities before me, not just shoplifting. I had a conscience, though. I still believed in God and karma and tried never to do things that would hurt people.

I bumped into Josh one day when I was twenty-eight. He was still on drugs and up to his same old tricks. He confessed that he got five hundred pounds for the chain he sold years back! How selfish to get that and only give Mum and me forty to share.

I soon knew all the smokers in South Norwood, and many visited Mum's. I was slightly timid back then; one day, my friend Lewis disrespected me. Then my older friend LP who was over ten years my senior and an ex-personal trainer backed me up. 'That's it; I've had enough of you disrespecting Duppy in his own house. Empty your pockets, now.'

'I'm sorry, LP.'

'It's Duppy you should be apologizing to. Empty your fucking pockets; I ain't telling you again.' LP then picked him up and turned him upside down, holding his ankles while shaking him. It looked like something from a cartoon. He literally shook his pockets empty, took his drugs, and then shared them with me. Lewis apologised, and LP wasn't heartless, so he gave him some too. That really cracked me up inside, and it felt nice having a mate stand up for me.

I'd go out at night, pull on car doors and get many items and money from the open ones. Within months, I'd tried almost every car within a few miles. Then, one night while walking in Crystal Palace, I spotted an open window, so I stood on a handrail and stuck my hand inside. I got a phone and a jewellery box containing silver. I sold the phone and some jewellery to the off-licence for twenty-something pounds. It was late, so I took whatever he offered. I sold the rest the next day for twelve pounds.

It only took a few days before the police identified my fingerprints and came to arrest me. Even though only my hand entered the property, I got charged with aggravated burglary. Aggravated because it was nighttime and the people were asleep inside. I found out I'd taken a five hundred pounds Tiffany bracelet, which I sold for four pounds. Back to HMP Thameside.

I requested a video link to court, as I'd be transferred to Highdown if I attended in person. So I settled in, became the wing barber, and got eighteen months reduced to twelve. I'd written a letter to the judge explaining the entire situation. After reading, he said to my solicitor, 'I think Mr Grossett has done your job for you here. Is there anything you would like to add?'

'No, I think he explained everything,' my solicitor replied.

TG Millian and Blanco from the Harlem Spartans drill group were on my wing; I cut TG's dreads off for him. This jail was fun; many people had iPhones, and sometimes we drank hooch. I eventually shared a cell with the biggest fish on the wing, who had ounces of spice. I'd never been so high in my life; we smoked 24/7. I was in prison, getting higher than I had on the road. I later discovered that the equality and diversity rep, Anita, was bringing it in for his cousin, Elijah. She got caught bringing him many iPhones and got a year in prison. She must've been in love with him because they exchanged thousands of love texts. A pretty officer named Tiana, whom I flirted with, eventually got caught bringing in 220g of cannabis and got three years and four months.

My mum once put me on the phone with her friend named Nicky. "Hi, I'm your mum's mate. She talks highly of you. It'll be nice to meet you when you get out."

I did my time, and Nicky was waiting at Mum's house to meet me upon release. But first, I went to a shop in Croydon and bought some spice, which was still a legal high. I smoked a spliff and was soon off my rocker, beating up a metal pole in Croydon. Many police and ambulance staff arrived, primarily female. I felt like I was in heaven. I have a crazy lust for nurses and police uniforms; it drives me wild. They took me to Mayday hospital, where I spent the night. Mum was so worried she visited me at 3am.

The next day I returned home and finally met up with Nicky. We smoked and got on well. We quickly became a couple; she was a traveller and we had a fun relationship. Two months in, my friend G visited me for a smoke, and I introduced him. Within a week, I discovered that Nicky had fallen for him, and they were together. He respectfully explained the situation so there wasn't bad blood. Why do my girlfriends always run off with my mates? This was another bitter pill to swallow because in some way, I loved all my partners. Again, I transmuted the pain with more crime and drugs. Every time I left jail with the best intentions, life constantly returned to the same as before; shoplifting and pulling on car doors.

My old smoking buddy, Jamie, visited once and had a bath, but we had no clean towels. Next thing, she was out and had a towel around her head.

'Where did you get that towel from?'

'Oh, it was in the bathroom.' The only towel in there was the one around the bottom of the toilet stopping the leaking, which was filthy and had been soaking up urine for weeks. I entered the bathroom and noticed it was missing. If you're that nasty to take that and put it on your skin, I'm saying nothing.

Mum had missed a court appearance for something minor, so she had a warrant out for her arrest. Then she and Brian had a drunken argument. He wouldn't leave, so Mum called the police.

'It's Good Friday and bank holiday Monday. If police come, you'll get arrested and be in until Tuesday,' I tell her.

"I don't fucking care; they can't arrest me. I want him gone."

'Please, Mum, don't do this.' She was adamantly set in her ways and never budged. I also had a warrant, so I left and watched from down the street.

The police arrived, handcuffed Mum and put her in the back of the car. Brian was smiling. A few minutes later, they handcuffed him too. I returned home, and the next day an officer came to collect Mum's medication. I hid at first, and Mike let him in; luckily, he was old, alone, and never knew me. I gave him Mum's huge box containing about a hundred boxes of pills.

Later that Saturday, Mum returned home. 'They saw all my medication and realized I was too unwell to spend four days in a cell, so they bailed me out.'

'How come Brian got arrested?'

'Well, when I saw him smiling, I thought fuck you bastard, you're getting nicked too. So I said he raped me. Ha-ha, who's laughing now?'

'That's bad, Mum. You can't say that.'

'Fuck him. I admitted I lied the next day, so they dropped the charges.'

Come Tuesday, Brian visited, looking like he'd just left a concentration camp. As an alcoholic, he must've suffered, enduring four days locked up without it.

'I told you, Brian, don't fuck with me; you'll never win,' Mum said.

Around September 2016, I saw a terrible accident on television. The reporter stated, 'A twenty-three-year-old man has admitted causing the deaths of a boy and his aunt, who were hit by a car being chased by police in south-east London in August. Joshua Dobby has denied manslaughter charges during a hearing at the Old Bailey.'

Oh my god, Josh had killed two people and injured three other children. He was escaping from the police, driving three times the speed limit, going down one-way roads and through red lights in Penge. He eventually mounted the pavement and crashed into this innocent family: devastating, heartbreaking news.

I was with him a few weeks before it happened and would've been in the car if I had been with him. He eventually pleaded guilty to manslaughter and death by dangerous driving. He got twelve years with an extra three on licence. Very sad indeed; my thoughts were with the victims. I wouldn't be seeing

Josh for a while.

I got arrested again for shoplifting and stealing two bikes. I got two months in jail. I was back in Highdown. G was there; his two friends, twins, whose faces I knew, were running the wing. One brother sold spice and must've made one hundred pounds a day for months. As the barber who cut all the top dogs' hair, I was looked after. People were also intrigued by how I could repeatedly hit metal poles with my arms. One female officer said I looked like a martial arts stripper. I read more scholarly books and left after two months.

Three days after my release, I bumped into a friend from jail. We scored and went to an electric cupboard in South Norwood to do our hits. He suggested I do all the twenty-pounds white and ten-pounds brown like he did. I thought it was a bit much, but I tried it. Oh my, this was too much, indeed. Everything went blurry. Then I saw some youngsters staring through the keyhole.

The day before, a friend, Beefy, was after me with a knife, making me think these kids wanted to stab me. I ran straight to South Norwood train station. My mate followed and got on the train, but paranoid me jumped off just before it left. I jumped on the train tracks, took my top off, and started rapping. I remember bigging up Lil Weezy and R.A., and people began filming. I wouldn't come off, and when the police arrived, I ran down the tracks. I kept going for a few hundred meters, climbed through gardens, and lay inside one for over an hour. Thankfully, the helicopter never spotted me; I escaped and found a shed to hide in. I searched the shed and found loads of bags containing clothes and stuff. I nicked three great-conditioned expensive trainers.

The next day I went home and continued as if nothing had happened. But a day later, my friend told me he had seen me in the newspaper. I also looked on YouTube to find embarrassing videos of me rapping on the train tracks. So, I rang my probation officer and told him what had happened.

I guessed I'd have another warrant shortly, so I called Twin in jail. 'Bro, I'm coming back soon. Can you sort out a parcel for me to bring in?'

'Duppy, my brudda, I'll pattern that up for you. Keep your phone on; I'll call you.' We agreed that he'll give me four ounces of spice and one hundred pounds. One ounce and the money for me, the rest for him.

When his girlfriend met me, she had the spice but only ten pounds. I took it but called and let him know that I was unhappy. I wasn't going into jail without any gear, and I needed the money for that. That Thursday, I never handed myself in. I knew I'd go to Thameside with Saturday court instead of Highdown, so I waited until Monday. I had the four ounces uncomfortably banked up my backside for five days.

On Tuesday, I scored with an associate who kept walking up the main roads. 'Oi bruv, I got a warrant; I can't be on these bait roads. I'm handing myself in, but I want a quick hit first.' A car then pulled up, and some plainclothes officers arrested me. Maybe it was good because I had the gear I hadn't used yet to take with me.

I got to Highdown Wednesday evening. The funny thing was that Thursday, the 17th of November 2016, was my twenty-ninth birthday. Twin smugly collected his parcel in the morning. I said hello to my comrades, who I'd only left eleven days before. I tried keeping quiet about my spice, but in jail, once one person knows, everybody does. So, we celebrated my birthday in style, and everyone got high. My mate later told me that it was humorous how the entire spur was empty that day as everyone was stoned in their cells. The few that came out stumbled around like zombies.

I sold some, but people talked, and after five days, the officers spun my cell. Of course, they never found anything on me as it was all banked. Still, I left one tiny spliff in some tissue under my mattress, which they found and stated fell off me when they strip-searched me.

'You liars. Why didn't you say something when it supposedly fell then?'

'Because we never wanted to cause a scene,' was their untrue reply. They knew it was mine, so they lied to ensure I got the punishment. They then put me on basic, so I had no TV and was only allowed out for half an hour with the few others on basic each day.

I shared a cell with a Scottish guy whose co-dee was secretly one of the biggest drug dealers in south London. He got found washing a kilo of coke down the drain because he unluckily left his metal reinforced door open. His paperwork showed the police had over three hundred different evidence samples of every narcotic going. He had a master key to every door lock, ordered drugs off the dark web, and delivered them to people's houses. All while disguised as a simple forklift driver.

We had a TV hidden in the cell, but it was pointless as we could hardly watch it; it was more headache than it was worth. I had a radio, luckily, and I smoked my spice all day and listened to music. The prosecution said my being on the train tracks cost the train service 1.5 million pounds in delays. The judge felt they were milking it a little, though.

I knew an Irish traveller who was on the other spur to me. We cut our bedsheets and swung lines to set up a pully system between our windows. We passed stuff back and forth at will. Usually, I gave him spliffs in return for food, as I had crazy munchies. The officers then found our TV and gave us another two weeks basic. We bought another, which also got found. Three were found in our cell altogether. The Senior Officer, Mr H, was an ex-nightclub bouncer and created reasons to keep us on basic for my whole sentence.

After two months, on the 16th of January, 2017, I was released. I stayed with Mum, who was living with her best friend, Clive. I was clean for four days until Nicky rang on the 21st, saying she was sick. So, I grafted, scored, and then met her at her friend's house, who lived directly opposite my mum's old flat.

'Nevaeh, this is my friend Duppy. Do you remember him from across the road? He's Lu-Lu's son. Can he stay with you for a few days?' She agreed and was incredibly kind.

I slept head-to-toe with Nevaeh because her friend was on the sofa. The next night we slept up on the same side. We kissed and stuff on the third day; you can imagine what happened on the fourth. Nevaeh became my new girlfriend; her kindness was attractive. Seven years my senior with two teenage children who lived with her family, she only smoked white but helped me with money sometimes. She had slight learning difficulties and young mental age, so she was delicately precious.

Things were going well, but a few weeks in, Nicky seemed jealous and thought she could win me back, thinking I'd choose her over Nevaeh; she was wrong. She even tried to get me beaten up over it. I moved in with Nevaeh, and her sister lived above us with her boyfriend. They also smoked; many people visited and smoked upstairs. I discovered that Nevaeh's dad owned the property and was a multi-millionaire living in a Spanish villa.

People said I was using her for sex, somewhere to stay, and money; I wasn't. I survived fine on my own. Numerous drug users visited, and life was relatively exciting and stable. However, Nevaeh's dad controlled her money. So, rather than her single large sums a few times a month, I proposed he averages it out, which worked out at thirty-five pounds a day. She got it at around 11:00am, which was perfect, as it was enough to get us our drugs. I really fell for Nevaeh, and people soon realised we were serious. But she hated Ariana Grande, who I was besotted with. I jokingly told her that Ariana was the only woman who, if she came along, I'd leave her for.

I'd missed court, so I had a warrant, but it didn't flag up for some reason. The warrant officers who hunted down wanted criminals knew me by name. They repeatedly looked for LP at ours and, surprisingly, said I wasn't wanted when name-checked. One was a hot blonde we fancied and preferred getting arrested by. They entered once amid us having sex. 'Don't worry, Dan, we're not here for you; you can continue in a sec.'

At this point, my world really started to change. When I did a snowball, a hit containing crack and heroin, reality started breaking at the seams. I could envision things, and they would essentially manifest around me to a degree. I couldn't just imagine anything and make it magically appear. But my mind could think of anything possible. That thought resonated and affected my reality with previously inexperienced energy, opening a new realm of unforeseen reality. Then, whatever thought I possessed in response to that new energy affected the reply.

My physiological makeup changed when I put this narcotic concoction in my body; it immediately altered my mentality. I could use that feeling it brought to influence my reality. It's tough to explain, but honestly, I'd do a hit outside, and the shadows of the trees started moving on their own. They directly responded to the energy I fed them. When sober, everything was normal. But after injecting these mind-altering chemicals into my body, the world around me would manifest all sorts of weird shapes and beings, not of this earth. They reacted to my thoughts, reflecting my every vibration with precision timing. Once, many demonic dog-type beings in the shadow realm swarmed around me and pushed me to the floor. I wondered, is this in my head? Was I going crazy? But it felt a thousand percent real.

24

Nevaeh/Trapping

I was grafting in Caterham one day; I was followed by a staff member out of the shop. He was on the phone with the police. I walked up a road next to the train station, which I never knew was over a mile long at the time. I spotted an Asian fella in a car, 'Yo, brother, I beg you drive me out of here. Some racist guys are chasing me.' I jumped in his car, and we drove back towards the station.

'That's him,' I said as we passed the guy following me. Then, an off-road truck appeared in front of us. They blast on their four huge spotlights and drive towards us. 'That's them, bro, please. They'll fuck me up if they get me.' I was unsure who they were but knew I must get away.

He reversed, crashing into multiple parked cars along the way. Then, finally, he spun around and drove fast to escape our chasers. 'I'll take you to the police station,' he said, as it was literally a minute's drive.

'No, please, don't.' We drove past the station, and he let me out. I quickly ran, hid, and heard the police searching with dogs. After an hour, I came out to find his car hitched on the side of a road. I realized that the car chasing us was the police, and they must've arrested him. I felt terrible because he was innocent, and they probably thought he was my accomplice. I returned home safely on the train but felt highly guilty as he may have been sitting in prison all because he helped me, a stranger.

In May, my father, Everton, was in hospital after suffering a cardiac arrest.

He was on a life support machine, and I was meant to say my goodbyes. But because of my lifestyle, I didn't. I will forever regret that. His funeral was later that month, but Damon didn't tell me about it until three weeks after it happened. I don't know what made him think that was OK, but I felt incredibly let down by him for doing that. Years later, he claimed he told me, but I'm adamant he didn't, as I sincerely don't remember it.

Later that month, I was a few doors down shouting through Janey's letterbox as Nevaeh was inside smoking. I'd been cutting electrical cables at home, so I had a 1cm lock-knife in my pocket. Suddenly, a police van pulls up. 'Excuse me, fella, what are you doing?'

'My friend lives here. I'm just calling through for her to open the door.'

'Well, you could be a burglar, so I'm gonna search you.' They found the blade and put me in cuffs. Then Nevaeh came out. These officers were from a different borough, so upon a namecheck, my warrant appeared. 'You do not have to say anything. But it may harm your defence if you do not mention, when questioned, something which you may later rely on in court. Anything you do say may be given in evidence.'

Nevaeh phoned Mum, who walked down from our house. I said my goodbyes and returned to prison. I got four months. Nevaeh visited, wrote, and sent me money. It was nice finally having a missus supporting me while inside. I did my time and returned home to score as usual. I still lived with Nevaeh, and life was fun. We smoked every day and hustled money in every way possible. I met a young dealer named Trizzy, who drove big foreign cars. We got on well and I bought off him sometimes. Nicky was still with G, and they'd regularly visit.

One day I was walking with Nicky, and we were completely broke. I mentioned that God is real, and everything I've ever prayed for had come true. She was secular and never really believed. 'Dan, if this God you believe in is so real, prove it. Believing in him ain't helping us right now, is it?'

'Okay, I'll give it a try. Please, God, we're in need. Please help us out of this situation somehow. Amen.' And halfway through saying amen, we spotted our friend at the cashpoint. We approached him, and he asked us to score saying he'd sort us out.

'Oh my God, Nicky, you saw that, right?'

'You know what, Duppy, I've never believed in God. But that was crazy; I saw it with my own eyes; it actually worked.'

I knew prayer worked, but that was the first time I'd experienced it so abruptly.

Nicky and G became homeless, so they moved into our front room. We all used drugs, so it was a hectic, constant merry-go-round. One day, G, who suffered delusions from taking drugs and not sleeping for days, got paranoid, thinking I fancied Nicky. Out of nowhere, he punched my face three times. I hit him back, and then LP broke it up. I shouted, 'What the fuck was that for? I ain't done shit wrong!'

'You like Nicky. I can tell.'

'I'm with Nevaeh. I'd be happy to never see Nicky again if I could.' I was disappointed, but I knew these were the bozos we had around us.

One night, G returned and pulled out three grand cash. 'I found a wallet in a car with many bank cards with pin numbers.' I ecstatically thought, yes, we'll all be having a good time tonight. But G never gave us a penny. He bought me one ten-pound bag of brown and gave Nevaeh nothing.

'Can you at least put some money on the electric meter?' we asked, but he didn't. He smoked all night, giving us a few pipes, and was paranoid, so I was scoring for him. He spent so much that the dealer accidentally gave me an extra forty-pound bit, which I kept until he left and was all I got out of it. I thought, what a slimy person to steal that amount and not give any to the people in whose house you stayed.

The next day, he and Nicky booked into a hotel, as they were scared that Beefy would take their money. So we thought, fuck them, keep it; at least it's got you out of our house. That same day I grafted ten pounds, so I asked G if he could sell me one-on-one, as he had bought an eighth of each. He agreed, and I met him at the Queen's Hotel in Crystal Palace.

We were walking to the shop when he spotted ten pounds on the floor, which he picked up. I then noticed another tenner in front of me. I went to get it when G barged me out of the way and grabbed it.

'Bro, we're meant to be on the same team. How are you gonna barge me? I would've acted differently if I knew it was like that.' While I was saying this, he spotted another tenner and ran and grabbed it. 'Rah, aren't you gonna split that thirty-pound?'

'If you snooze, you lose,' he replied. How low can you be to have three grand, knowing how hard it is for us to make even a tenner, and give me none of the money we had just found. We went to the shop, where I even gave him twenty pence towards a drink as he stated he never had change. I thought, you snake, you'll get your karma one day.

Nevaeh soon stated that if I was smoking brown, she also wanted to. I dissuaded her, but she started smoking it behind my back. Nevaeh developed an addiction, so we'd both be sick without it. Before, she was relatively normal, but drugs dominated our lives from that point.

That November, I got put on a tag for three months. So, I couldn't go out after 7:00pm. One month in, we ran out of electricity and noticed the tag box turned off. They're meant to have a forty-eight-hour backup battery, but mine seemed broken. When it turned back on, we never got a phone call from the tag company, so Nevaeh suggested I go out and see what happened. I unplugged it and then went out briefly. Upon my return, still no phone call. So, for the next two months, I turned my tag box off whenever I wanted to go out after seven. When the people came to retrieve it, they looked at each other, mentioning it was faulty. I acted as if I had never known its relevance but cheekily smiled.

Soon, a young dealer named Rahiem returned from prison and started selling again. He offered us a deal to sell drugs from our house for three rocks a day. We agreed. He did it briefly and then recruited LP to work for him. So, LP moved into our front room and sold drugs. Finally, we had what we constantly needed around us, making life easier. Also, when people bought it, they shared it with us. Our house became a bando. Users were constantly around; it was exciting but sometimes stressful without much privacy.

Rahiem regularly paid me a few stones to help him bag up. So we'd be sitting in Janey's flat a few doors down, bagging up like four hundred deals, which took hours, making my hands ache. He progressed from an eighth up to probably a quarter of a kilo. He cooked crack well, and it was funny when he got high off the fumes.

We noticed an old-school Brixton crackhead named Simon bought white, then went to our immediate neighbour's doorway and smoked it. We lived on the main road, and this was indiscreet. So, Rahiem put some crack on the table, 'Oi, Simon, come take this.' Simon smilingly reached for it. Bang! Rahiem punched him. 'Why the fuck are you smoking outside the house? Are you tryna get me nicked? Come, take it.'

'Dada, please don't punch me.'

'Take the fucking stone.' He punches him again. He sold him the rock, stating, 'If you ever smoke outside again, I'll stop serving you and fuck you up.' We laughed after he left.

Another time Rahiem shouted, 'This is my bando!' I thought fuck you, this is our flipping house, mate.

Mum soon became very unwell from her illness. She'd stopped taking her medicine and had given up on life. Damon suggested something like taking colloidal silver, eating certain other products, and having positive thoughts could heal her. Yes, I totally agreed with him to an extent; good energy is beneficial beyond understanding. But I also respect science, and doctors know what they're doing; take medicine if it's saving your life. Damon was always the backbone and responsible member of our family, but this was advice I disagreed with.

Mum was terribly ill and dropped to under seven stone in weight. She was in Mayday hospital and almost died; seeing her made us all cry. I'd visit her, and when her health started improving, I'd take her downstairs in a wheelchair for cigarettes, as she couldn't go alone. The one thing Mum wanted, though, was a pipe of white. I tried dissuading her, but I loved her dearly and did whatever I could to make her happy. I'd score; we'd sneak to a blind spot outside and have a quick smoke. She'd start chatting away after her pipe, and I'd wheel her back upstairs. I would've begged her to do the same if I were in her position.

25

Higher Dimensions

Narcotics highly affected my reality. Whenever I did a snowball, my mind interacted with higher dimensions. The shadows I had been interacting with over the previous months were evolving. I'd literally see all sorts of monsters in people's shadows. When we're influenced by substances, our altered perception changes how we perceive reality. And my altered mental state manifested itself in my existence. I discovered that there really are higher dimensions that our spirit can interact with and influence. Our soul has no limits; it can influence many dimensions, as it is not limited by physicality.

A central component that affected me was equal and opposite. With drugs, your entire reality changes magically and immediately; its abilities lie in that altered feeling. Influenced by narcotics, my emotions differed from when sober. I realised that I could say a word or think a thought, and the notion would create new energy containing equal and opposite. Because my mind was altered by the substances, it made totally different energy than when sober. And the universe, via the shadow realm above our physical dimension, manifested and evolved that opposition right before me. It then incited a new emotion, like the Fibonacci developed energy of my original thought.

As I sought an enlightening path towards nirvana, the dark shadow realm was essentially manifesting hell. But I understood that it only reacted to what I fed into it. It automatically went further down its desired path, which was my opposite. As I sought the light, it sought darkness. The purer my thoughts were when high, the eviler the demonic shadows became. It's simple polarities – and everything has them - even in spiritual realms. In hindsight, I believe this polarity helped propel me further into enlightenment. As far as your polar opposite takes you, you must answer with an even stronger opposing force.

Soon, the three stones a day from Rahiem dropped to one. And eventually, he gave us nothing. The audacity of these youngsters was crazy, and they sometimes saw us smokers simply as junkies. I used drugs, but I was never a crackhead. There's a significant difference between a drug user and a crackhead. I still kept my principles and some self-pride. Being around the drugs was exciting; there was always something happening. Rahiem sent me to the country with three hundred deals worth around two grand to drop off with his worker. But sometimes, if I had a parcel, I'd be tempted to use some.

Another time I took way more than I was meant to, and Damon gave me three hundred pounds to pay Rahiem off. He wasn't someone to mess with, so I thank Damon sincerely for saving my ass. One time, I got a few slaps after smoking what I wasn't meant to. But generally, we were a great team with the best drugs line in the area.

In May 2018, I used drugs for days without sleep and went into some of the darkest realms I'd ever entered. I felt I'd crossed over into hell and was its most powerful entity. Because I felt heavenly feelings of extreme pleasure when high, I believe the universe replied with the equal and opposite feeling. As I sought heaven and had total faith in God, the devil seemed to be the only adversary. I directly experienced both polarities. I felt I controlled the perplexities of heaven and hell to a degree. The stronger my pleasurable emotions and experiences were in our reality, the darker I became in the opposite. My friends, who weren't skilful magicians, weren't as powerful in hell because this was my creation; my mind had created this realm. So, therefore, I was most prominent.

Because of opposites, I was the devil, the most potent ambassador in hell. This energy was the opposite of what I felt in reality, so the purer and more perfect I tried to be, the more powerful I became in hell. If I analysed the moment, seeing the most demonic creations imaginable and attempted to increase that power with an evil thought, it only weakened my dark abilities. That wasn't my responsibility to control those creations; it was the universe's job, manifesting my opposite. I sought heaven, happiness, and love. And the more I felt heaven, the stronger I became as the devil. I could control how powerful the dark shadows manifested by experiencing more pleasure. So again, I understood that this was all based on equality and opposition. I created and was experiencing this, so I had to fulfil it.

I was high in my room with Nevaeh and Nicky and misused the word 'Insha'Allah,' which in Arabic means 'if Allah wills it.' Upon saying it, three pitch-black humanoid shadow figures abruptly landed in the room. I immediately noticed an incredible look of shock and terror on Nicky's face, highlighting that she had seen something too. I was shocked at my words' power and knew I was playing with unfathomable energies.

I did a snowball on the third day and went far into another dimension. I saw a tiny alien in the corner of the room, which didn't look like any of the ones you see in movies. Instead, it was a little greenish circle around the size of a plum, with two eyes staring directly at me. The only thing that kept me sane was my faith. I knew God created all things, so everything is under his authority. And my trust in him was more potent than any fear of his creations

Upon entering this darkest of realms, the only thing I could do to keep myself safe was to call God's name. So, being scared that I might lose my life or my sanity, in my fear, I called out, 'Allah!' The dimension I had entered immediately evolved ten times deeper upon calling his name. Maybe because I had entered the most powerful thing in existence into the equation. And this magical universal energy directly fed off what I fed into it, words included. I was in a far scarier place than before. So, I called again the only name I knew was powerful enough to save me, 'Allah!' I then went another ten levels more profound into the realm I was just in. This was the scariest place I'd ever been

Imagine feeling something and then feeling that exact emotion tenfold. Then feeling that same more profound emotion enhanced again to the power of ten. And the second evolution of the power of ten is one hundred times the original factor, which only increases. This was not a happy place; it was the opposite. Nine times this happened, I called out to God, 'Allah!' and went unimaginably deeper. Then, upon the tenth time, I heard and felt a bang directly in front of me. A burst of energy like a mini big bang of creation, but this was in a different dimension right before me. I was dripping in sweat, with Nevaeh by my side. I felt ashamed and impure, calling the lord's name while high. But I also felt that something incredibly profound had just happened.

Everyone around me immediately acted differently. Is reality all created within our own minds? Because everything and everyone seemed to have been affected by this bang. I had also lost any fear, as I'd been to my darkest place, which then evolved tenfold. And another tenfold, nine times.

In hindsight, I understood the mathematics and energy of what had happened. When I called Allah, I brought God's power into the equation, which increased what I was experiencing to its maximum potential. And tenfold is the maximum increase before you return to zero and restart the count. And upon this happening nine times, the small explosion or bang happened because the tenth was the last point of possibility. You cannot increase tenfold the energy of God ten times. It was too much energy for this reality to handle because that would be one hundred percent, so it imploded. So, still alive after experiencing such a terrifying experience, I feared nothing.

Later that day, Nevaeh and I had a huge argument. She rang the police and, as usual, started talking rubbish. They already had it twice on their file of her calling them, lying, and then admitting it days later. She left the house and was still on the phone around the corner.

'Nevaeh, please don't do this; I'll get arrested.'

'Get the fuck away from me; I don't care.'

'Please, Nevaeh.'

I was about to jump on my bike when two police officers arrived. One handcuffed one hand, then Nevaeh whispered, 'They're already dead.'

With everything I'd experienced regarding different dimensions, her statement made me believe these officers weren't even human anymore, so I punched one. I almost got them off of me, but they overpowered me.

'Right, you're under arrest for assault on a PC too.' At the station, they refused my bail because my bail address was Nevaeh's house, and she was the complainant. So I was remanded to jail.

I landed in Thameside again and knew a few faces. I disinfected my cell from top to bottom and settled in. After two weeks, a mate from Croydon arrived, so we banged up together. I felt comfortable around a friend I trusted rather than a stranger. I was soon cutting hair, and life was good. Then, a month in, a solicitor visited me. 'What case are you to do with?' I ask.

'I'm here regarding your father's estate.' He notified me that I'd inherited twenty grand and explained accessing it. Wow, this wasn't bad at all. My father worked hard his whole life; his family should get anything he left behind.

I went back ecstatic, and my solicitor sent me fifty pounds a week for my entire sentence. I bought a quarter of a page of spice, as it was then sprayed onto letters and sent straight in. I got super high in my cell every evening. Tobacco was no longer allowed in prisons, so we'd use teabags mixed with melted-down nicotine patches instead. They actually tasted nice, and I almost preferred them to cigarettes.

I met a martial arts instructor on the wing with five different black belts two months in. My cellmate had changed, and his cellmate was a loser. So, I mentioned that I had money and asked if he could share my cell and teach me. He agreed; this was my dream come true.

He taught me everything he knew and the principles, defining that being honourable and noble was vital. He also taught me healing aspects. 'The last jail I was in, I shared a cell with another martial arts instructor for two years; we taught each other daily. The officers also got us in the gym to teach them all the locks and stuff,' he said.

I was grateful to be there; it became another time when destiny blessed me through disguise. I felt like Danielson in *The Karate Kid*, Rocky in the mountains, or Frank Dux from *Kickboxer* in the jungle. A few months in, I was in court for a separate matter. Since remanded, I hadn't spoken to Mum as she'd changed her number. I was in the cells waiting when I heard her familiar voice. I shouted, 'Louise, Mum, it's Daniel.'

'I can hear someone calling me. Is that my son? Dan!' Mum hollered. I pressed the bell.

'Oi jailer, that's my mum out there. I haven't spoken to her for two months; can I please say hello?'

Mum had gotten a fine in court after another fight with Brian. Luckily, they let me sit privately with her for ten minutes. Wow, Mum had been in court literally twice in her life, and what were the odds that the exact day I was there, she was there too? I sincerely thanked God for manifesting this miracle for me.

My money ensured that my sensei and I had the best time possible, as this was a once-in-a-lifetime opportunity. To share a cell with an instructor who taught me for a few hours every day. Life was heaven; God had truly blessed me.

'You might've been an easy wrap-up when I met you, but you definitely aren't now,' he told me.

I bought five pages of spice for four hundred pounds at a time and lived like a king with seventy-pound canteens weekly. I had a laundryman job, so I was out of my cell all day. I also did the peace education course for the second time.

One day on the twice-a-week course, I was singing upstairs. A pretty teacher outside was smiling at me, basically dancing. This continued for five minutes, and all the other prisoners shouted, 'She's feeling you, bruv,' and 'You're in there.'

When she came up, we caught eyes and had a spark. So the next week, I came and sang another song, and I directed it at her. The following week, the same. Her name was Alex. I sang the entire Rihanna 'What's My Name,' but replaced it with, 'Oh, na na, Alex is her name,' in front of about seven teachers and plenty of prisoners. She was flattered.

It was summer, and she even started wearing her own pretty clothes instead of her uniform to work. The cleaner who worked with her daily told me, 'Bro, she's doing that for you. I've seen her for months, and she's never done this before.'

Every meet, we flirted. I told Alex I'd sing her a song every week until I went home. She became my thrilling obsession, helping me through this sentence.

I was living the dream even though I was in prison. I felt freer in jail since outside, I was a prisoner of drugs, completely controlling my freedom. So inside, I got to be the real me without addiction directing my actions.

On the 24th of October 2018, after five months on remand, I had my day in court. Nevaeh wasn't in the country or pressing any charges, as I'd literally done nothing wrong. So, my solicitor advised me if I pleaded guilty to common assault, I'd get to go home today, so I did.

Then I found out Nevaeh had requested a restraining order. This didn't make sense because we'd been in contact throughout the sentence.

I got out and met Mum right away. We smoked, and I stayed with her at her bed and breakfast in Croydon. The next day, Nevaeh met me.

'Why did you put a restraining order on me?'

'It wasn't me; I didn't even answer the phone. It was my sister.'

'Well, that was stupid. We can't legally talk or see each other for five years.'

'Oh, don't worry about it, Daniel.' Nevaeh had moved to Snodland in Kent and lived with her sister and two greyhound-cross-staff puppies. I still had over ten grand left, so I bought all new clothes and electrical goods. Trying to be positive, I smoked my drugs instead of injecting them.

This quiet little village was completely different from London. With my first two dogs who I loved, a three-bedroom house, and money, life was a fairy tale. Nevaeh knew the few local smokers, and we'd score from a youngster named Benny, who dealt from her friend Jack and Maria's house. I spent around two hundred pounds a day. I also discovered the rapper Giggs lived about a ten-minute walk around the corner.

Having a smartphone, I searched on Facebook for my siblings, Tyreese and Tiana. A page appeared of a boy named Tyreese; at first sight, he looked like family. So I messaged him, saying we might be brothers if his mother's name was Louise Willison.

I turned thirty-one that November and life was sweet. But my mental state went deeper and deeper into unknown realms. This was when the most powerful experiences of my life began happening. When I got high, my shadow started moving on its own, doing all sorts of things. It seemed that the shadows I'd been interacting with all that time had evolved enough to manifest their own creations. But as I understood it, the shadow realm manifested opposite my desire. I felt this was because everything has an equal and opposite. So, when I got high and felt ultimate pleasure, it created the opposite energy.

For example, I'd smoke and then see my shadow without a head. Or I'd see all types of strange alien animal things, usually attached to my body. These were living and moving entities that were nothing of this earth. Nevaeh and I would be sitting in my room, and in my peripheral vision, I'd clearly see my shadow moving on its own. Or I'd see my shadow on the wall; I'd be totally still and notice it turn its head and look at me. But it wasn't just in my mind; Nevaeh saw the same thing I did every time. Every day this happened immediately after putting narcotics in my body.

Just as we can physically touch and affect things around us, we can also affect things with our minds. And our minds are not physically limited, so we can interact with the entire universe with a thought, as it's all connected through dark energy.

'Nevaeh, you can see my shadow moving on its own, right?'

'Yes, Daniel, it's got no head,' she'd reply.

I tested it dozens of times by witnessing what I saw, not saying anything, and asking Nevaeh what she saw. And she'd precisely describe what I'd seen. So it essentially became a severe game where my faith was tested by seeing how dark an experience I could bear. I really had truly alien entities attached to my body, focusing on me. But I never ever doubted my creator.

Many times I considered recording it for proof. My best explanation of why I didn't is this. Imagine holding on to the tallest building in the world with both hands. You desperately want a picture, but you might fall and die if you reach for the camera in your pocket. Every time I experienced this, it took every part of my spirit to keep God in my heart and not let these alien beings overcome me. I desperately wanted proof, but keeping my soul and not dying or going to hell by having these powerful entities overtake me was more important than attaining evidence.

It was a scary territory, but I also felt privileged that I was the one chosen to experience it. We are the latest thing the universe offers. Hence, it's up to us to achieve the most astonishing things it has ever experienced. Our spirit is above the physical realm. I believe we all come from one spirit: the spirit of God, our creator. So, we are all connected through it. I wasn't sure who or what was controlling what my shadow did. I felt it may have been the universe itself, discovering itself through me. Then again, it may have been me, through experiencing utmost pleasure and therefore creating the opposite energy, as it simply manifested the opposite of what I felt.

My feelings were extremely pleasurable when I was high. Drugs release the same endorphins we get upon feeling pleasure, so it's an unhealthy hack into feeling good. When I felt that great, it created an equal and opposite feeling somewhere else. The shadows exposed and manifested that opposite feeling. I felt heaven, so those shadows seemed to express hell. It's all to do with balance. When specific energy is manifested or experienced, the opposite must also be embodied to keep stability. What I saw wasn't just in my head; it manifested in this reality, the shared matrix we are all a part of.

26

Snodland, Kent

After two months, my money had run out, so I sold my brand-new laptop, TV, stereo, keyboard, and PlayStation 4 for less than a quarter of what I'd paid. I'd spent roughly five grand with Benny, yet he wouldn't even let me off a few pounds when I was broke. I thought, you cheeky bastard, I spent all that and now you treat me like shit and leave me sick. So, I returned to crime.

There were two local shops that I stole from for months, taking all their champagne and wine and then selling it to a shop across the road. I also pulled on car doors at night and found that many people had left their doors unlocked in this quiet village. So I pulled on every car; finding all sorts of stuff was a thrill. I felt guilty, though, knowing the problems I caused. It's a miserable existence grafting money from nothing and getting sick every day. But when I had my drugs, it all felt worth it.

Our dogs grew big, and I loved them like family. It was lovely having our own peaceful house without constant visitors like in London. Then, however, life became tougher because Nevaeh's dad started charging me fifteen pounds daily to stay there. He took it directly from her money. So she only got forty pounds every other day. We had to find money on the days without it, as we hardly saved gear for them.

One day I had cocaine. I injected it because I never knew how to wash it into crack. This got me back injecting from that day. I entered a car one night and found five hundred pounds in foreign notes, three laptops, four smartphones, and some other stuff. I made roughly two grand from that one.

I soon discovered that the house my father owned, which was in my brother's and my name, was no longer ours. Dad had met a woman four years before he passed away, and they changed his tenancy to a joint one. So, upon his death, she sold his house for hundreds of thousands of pounds and bought herself a new car. She wasn't invited to his funeral. I was upset, but I also knew that the greatest gift my dad had left was inside of me. We can always buy another house, but we cannot change our DNA and who we are.

In July 2019, I got a two-month suspended sentence for eight counts of shoplifting. The funny thing was, I got bailed to the same house as Nevaeh. My restraining order was never mentioned. Then on the 6th of August, I got one year and two weeks for fourteen charges of interfering with motor vehicles.

I landed in HMP Elmley, my new local prison. It was designed identically to Highdown and Belmarsh, so it felt familiar. Luckily, I had banked a few ounces of tobacco, as you couldn't smoke in jails anymore. So I sold some for spice and was comfortable for a while.

Upon landing on the detox wing, I spotted a beautiful officer, 'Hi, what's it like here?'

'They're very needy.' Her name was Miss Martin. There were many pretty officers here, a real treat for the eyes. I became comfortable and took over as barber as usual. But I really fell for Miss Martin. She had beautiful blue eyes and was the most attractive woman I'd ever seen. I didn't mind being in jail because I got to see her. I moulded myself, trying to be the male energy of her aura. I'd never been attracted to anyone this much, and seeing her in uniform did it for me. I spoke to her whenever possible and had a couple of long conversations; I was besotted.

My cellmate mentioned that Stefflon Don's brother, the rapper Dutchavelli was here; he'd seen him every morning attending his trial. Nevaeh wrote and visited me a few times; the restraining order never affected us.

Before I left, I told Miss Martin, 'I'm gonna make it in life and come back for you.' Yes, I had a girlfriend I loved, but I'd never denied my true feelings.

In February 2020, I went home to Nevaeh, who had drugs waiting for me

Jack and Maria had lost their flat, so they stayed in our spare room. We argued two days later as Nevaeh had eaten all the food and given the rest to the dogs. Then she called the police. Upon noticing her on the phone with them, I tried to take it out of her hand. 'Help me, help me. He's attacking me. I'm scared,' she yelled.

'She's lying. I haven't touched her. Check her file; she always does this.' I'd never hit a woman.

Police would probably be coming, and even though I'd done nothing wrong, I was still on a licence, the second half of your prison sentence. I knew that I might get recalled. If you're on a licence, anyone can create a lie, and even if they admit they lied, you'll still go back to prison most times if you're arrested. So, I quickly packed a bag and left.

I returned home the next day. 'Nevaeh, what happened?'

'Oh, nothing. The police came and asked a few questions, then left.'

'You know I could go back to prison for this. What did you say?'

'Nothing; I told them nothing happened.' Maria confessed that Nevaeh gave a statement accusing me of criminal damage for opening my own door and supposedly pushing her. If she only knew how detrimental her actions would eventually be.

'Nevaeh, I didn't touch you. You're meant to love me; how could you do this again?'

'I'm sorry, Daniel, forget about it.'

'No, you need to sort this out. You need to tell the truth.'

'I will. I'll call them tomorrow.'

The next day I phoned my probation officer, explaining everything. 'Miss, I didn't do anything wrong. Please don't recall me. It's not fair that I go to prison because someone lies.'

'Depending upon what happens, we'll go from there. But ultimately, if it's proven you've done nothing wrong, you shouldn't go back to prison.'

We returned to using drugs daily, with me repeatedly reminding Nevaeh to call the police to confess her lies. But the struggle of hustling money daily for heroin always became the first priority. The shadows were manifesting as alien beings, as usual. It became such a norm that seeing incredible strange creatures on my body in my shadow just became an everyday part of life. When I put these chemicals in my body and interacted with higher dimensions, the beings in those realms felt my power, so they attracted me. I also wondered if that previous explosion had sent energy across the universe, and maybe these beings were coming towards the source of it.

It was scary. Imagine seeing your shadow with unearthly animals attached to your body. Yet, when you look at your body, there's nothing there. So, I figured they may have cloaking devices or be in higher dimensions. Humans can only see about 0.0035% of the electromagnetic spectrum, known as visible light. Therefore, there could be many entities within different wavelengths we cannot see. But none could overcome the fact that light couldn't penetrate them, so their shadow was there.

We had huge mirrors on our wardrobe in our room, and when high, I'd envision things mentally and sometimes see them in the mirror if I focused. A mirror can open a fantasy realm with different potentialities from the real world. Essentially, it's a mirrored reality, so I could use that medium to create things beyond the laws of our natural world.

I believe the universe is God manifest, so we're all a tiny part of God, and any component can do God's work. And I was definitely doing many things beyond modern human understanding and comprehension. I'd walk down the street and see regular people going about their lives, thinking, wow, if you only knew what's possible, what's genuinely happening behind closed doors.

I kept in touch with probation, and life continued. After two weeks, the police phoned me, stating that I wasn't in trouble but needed to do an interview. The next day I attended Maidstone police station.

'This police station is closed, so we'll take you to Tonbridge. Therefore, we must arrest you, but you're not in trouble.'

They interviewed me, and I told the truth; I didn't do anything. Afterwards, the sergeant stated, 'Daniel Grossett, the good news is you're being bailed; the bad news is you've been recalled to prison.'

'Huh, you're joking. I only spoke to my probation officer yesterday; this isn't fair.' Probation had recalled me two days after the incident and hadn't told me even though we had spoken for two weeks.

I landed back in Elmley feeling incredibly disheartened. I was only out for twenty days and was back inside with the same inmates I'd left behind.

'Grossett, I didn't think I'd see you again,' Miss Martin stated.

'My girlfriend lied and said I pushed her; I've been recalled. Hopefully, it's only fourteen or twenty-eight days.'

"Sounds like a toxic relationship."

I felt like a right fool. So much for making it and coming back for her. Back inside, I was cutting hair and chasing spice, as it always takes a while to get on your feet. The police decided no further action regarding Nevaeh's lies. Hopefully, I'd be out soon, as that was the reason for my recall.

Two weeks in, my probation officer visited. 'We feel a full recall is appropriate, as it seems you have serious issues regarding this vulnerable female.'

'Are you serious? I didn't do anything wrong and that's been proven. This isn't fair. What have I legally done wrong?"'

'Well, it's not that simple; many factors are involved.'

'What's your reason on paper for recalling me?'

'The victim is vulnerable, and we must consider her welfare.'

'There was no victim; the charges got dropped! Wasn't a twenty-eight-day recall sufficient? For legally doing nothing wrong? This isn't fair. You know what? My heart is clean; I'll ride the time. Just know, karma comes for us all, including you.'

I couldn't believe it; I had to serve out the other half of my sentence, another six months. All because Nevaeh lied. And even after the charges were dropped, probation kept me in jail.

The next day I got shipped to a C-cat prison named Rochester. Upon landing there, I spotted a mate from Elmley, 'Yes, Duppy. Barber man's here; I can get a decent trim now.' He introduced me to his mates and promoted my excellent barbering skills.

I banged up with someone who also came from Elmley with me. He smoked some spice and then started spazzing out on his bed. I thought, rah, this stuff looks strong; I'm gonna do a small amount. So I just lay on my top bunk. Then he started acting fruity. 'Oi, can't you wank me off? I'm bisexual. Please, I won't tell anybody.' Nobody had tried homosexual behaviour on me in all ten prisons on roughly forty sentences before.

'No, bruv, I'm straight; I'm good. Stop, please, allow it.' He pestered for a minute but eventually got the point.

I did two haircuts each day that weekend and was everyone's favourite new prisoner. But, unfortunately, it was the induction wing, so I'd soon get moved unless I found a permanent cell. Luckily, a friend found one for me, so I moved in with Foley on Monday. I settled in, and he bought an A4 sheet of the most potent spice I'd ever smoked. One square centimetre would've lasted me all night. He gave me a tiny bit, then got high all night. The next day he asked me, 'Have you got a pipe for me, mate?'

'Huh, what happened to your page?'

'It's finished.'

'You did a whole page in one day. Wow, you're a beast; that would've lasted me months.' So I shared the bit he gave me with him for the next week.

The virus called COVID-19 scared the whole world, and two weeks into my sentence, the UK went into lockdown. This affected jails also, so the entire regime changed. We were all locked in our cells for over twenty-three hours a day. No movements, work, or education severely disrupted the jail's routine No one could easily acquire drugs anymore, and the prices slowly increased outrageously. Rochester was a C-cat, so usually, there were drugs galore. But we were locked in our cells all day; they only let out a quarter of the wing at a time. Time really dragged, but we got used to it eventually. At the start of the sentence, Mum had sent me twenty pounds. She mentioned that her throat was sore, and her voice was slightly croaky. She felt she might have cancer.

27

Rest In Peace Mum

I hated my probation officer for how she betrayed me. I phoned her and said, 'Imagine if I lied about you and you got punished. Imagine I told your manager you tried to touch me during our meetings, and then you had to stop work while it was investigated. How'd you feel?' She reported that statement to her managers; thankfully, they changed her. My new male officer was sweet as a nut.

I shared a cell with a guy who farted literally every two minutes, hundreds of times a day, and they stunk! I got high and thought I was in hell. Another cellmate regularly swallowed air and then burped fifty times in a row; it almost caused us to fight. One showered but never scrubbed his feet. I'd be eating my dinner and smelling cheesy foot. Another inmate bet me ten pounds that it took over two years for light from the sun to reach earth. I said I'd studied many books and was obsessed with the universe; it takes about eight minutes. Weeks later, I showed him proof in a book and told him to keep the money.

Because I'd been recalled for no reason, I tried every way possible to get out. Finally, my probation officer said if I could provide an address, I could get released early on a tag. Mum put me in contact with her friend Mark, and the address was accepted. My probation officer, personal officer, and the prison governor recommended my release. But the decision-makers refused, stating I needed to work on my attitude towards females. What a load of horse shit. I only had one common assault against a female when Nevaeh lied, but

I pleaded guilty to it just to get out of prison. And how could I work on my supposed attitude when prisons are all in lockdown because of the virus, so no courses were running?

I tried phoning Mum repeatedly but got no answer. Then, one day I called my brother Alex, who told me that Damon had been charged with attempted murder and was in prison for stabbing somebody. That was shocking, as Damon had never been in trouble and was always responsible. Alex never said too much but stated that the victim wasn't hurt badly.

One Sunday, a few weeks later, I called Mum, and Alex answered. 'I'm with Mum, bro; it's not looking good.'

'What do you mean? What's happened?'

'Cancer; she's in a bad way and can't speak. They're saying Mum's only got a few months left. She hasn't eaten for two weeks.

'Can't she drink her Ensure?'

'No, she has a tumour in her throat; you can see it through her mouth. She's worse than before. Mum's tryna stay alive for you and Damon; when she could talk, she mentioned all she wanted was to see you both.'

'Put me on loudspeaker, please.'

'Mum, I love you. You're the best mum this world has ever offered. Sorry, I can't be there, but I'll be out soon. You've got me, Damon, Alex, Tyreese, and Tiana, your beautiful children. No one can ever take away the times we shared. I'm gonna make it in life. Please stay strong, Mum; I love you.'

Then I heard Mum say, 'Not even a tear,' as loud as if she said it herself. I burst into tears and continued telling my mum how much I loved her. I later contemplated how I clearly heard my mother speak, even though she couldn't physically. I believe her emotion at that time was powerful enough to transcend physicality for me to hear her. That evening my cellmate comforted and supported me. I told the officers, the chaplain, and probation the next day.

'I've only got two months left. You're letting people out eight weeks early because of Covid. I'm in jail over nothing, and my mum is dying of cancer. Is there nothing that can be done?' They were very supportive and tried their best, but what could they do?

That Monday night, I spoke with Alex and Mum again. And again on Tuesday. The chaplain arranged a phone call for me in their office on Wednesday morning.

'It's not good news, bro. She went last night.' My mum passed away on the 16th of June 2020. I cried again and told the officers. A lovely one named Miss Daniels comforted me and gave me a hug.

I returned to my cell and didn't know what to think or feel. I was most upset that I didn't get to say goodbye in person. We had lived together for almost twenty-eight years and were best friends. We all must die one day, but the fact I never got to look into Mum's eyes and tell her that I loved her killed me inside. I was in prison all because someone had lied. I love you, Mum; you're my angel. You will forever be with me in spirit and live on through us, your children.

Mum's funeral was on the 11th of August. I attended with two prison officers, handcuffed to one of them. When Mum was alive, we heard a beautiful song called 'Sleep Song' by Secret Garden. She had asked for that to be her funeral song. So, I begged Alex to please fulfil that one request. The beautiful thing was that the song's chorus sings, 'lu li lu lai lay,' and Mum's nickname was Lu-Lu, so it was perfect. It's the song I want for my funeral too. I gave a beautiful speech that Mum would've been proud of. But Damon wasn't there.

I was released from prison on the 18th of August and given a hotel reservation for two weeks. Nevaeh met me immediately and was clean. She'd been evicted from her house as Jack and Maria brought drug dealers around and violently robbed them, creating a crime scene. I bought some alcohol and spice but never scored any class A like every other time.

Losing Mum changed me, and I wanted to make her proud. I thought that if I died right then and there, I'd feel like I'd wasted my life. So, I prioritised trying to change my life and sticking with it this time. We couldn't find the hotel, so I stayed in Maidstone at Nevaeh's new bedsit. But the next day we found it and we stayed there instead. We smoked cigarettes in the room, as I didn't know you couldn't smoke inside them.

The next day, the police turned up, so Nevaeh quickly jumped into the bath. 'You're not in trouble; we're just checking up on those who have recently left prison. So, who's your guest?'

'I'm not under arrest, and my guest doesn't know I have a criminal history. Can you please leave?' They wanted to talk to my guest but eventually left. Later, the hotel staff kicked me out for smoking in the room.

Luckily, while walking through Maidstone town, I saw an old mate named Carlos, who I gave twenty pounds to stay with for a few days. I told probation where I was staying. The next morning, the police knocked on the door. 'Daniel Grossett, you're under arrest for breach of a restraining order.' They'd checked the hotel's CCTV and realized that I was with Nevaeh, who I legally couldn't contact. I went to court and was given a fine. I stayed with Carlos for a few weeks; he was an active injecting addict. I smoked a few odd crack pipes and bought one bag of brown. After smoking half of it, I realized this was no longer for me. So, I gave it to Carlos and vowed never to use heroin again.

I got housed in Lilysmith House hostel in Maidstone town centre in October. It was a lovely room with a shower, bathroom, and shared kitchen facilities. I finally had somewhere to live again. Because I wasn't feeding a heroin addiction, I lived comfortably for the first time ever. That November, I turned thirty-three.

Having a smartphone I hadn't sold, I caught up on many world affairs and the latest music I'd missed over the years while focusing solely on drugs. A Chiraq rapper named King Von was fatally shot; his music became my favourite.

I stayed clean from hard drugs but replaced them with smoking spice. I became addicted and needed it daily; otherwise, I'd be sick. I never returned to crime but relied on Nevaeh as she lent me ten pounds every other day, and I paid her back monthly. Where she lived was staffed, and one staff member was a militant ex-police officer. He knew about the restraining order, so I couldn't visit or be seen with her. However, we'd regularly meet in parks, and she sometimes stayed at my place.

I also saw another incident that broke my heart. My Vauxhall Primary School friend, Jahreau Shepherd, had become a great MMA fighter nicknamed 'The Nightmare.' But on the 11th of July 2020, while celebrating his thirtieth birthday party, he was brutally stabbed to death by his half-brother. We played football daily together as kids. It was very sad indeed. I didn't know what direction to go, but my hostel linked me with charities who bought me a laptop and barbering equipment. I had everything necessary, including expensive hair clippers, so I considered becoming a mobile barber and set up an Instagram page.

I also discovered online porn. Wow, I'd never had a chance or the technology to see those things all those years. So I definitely caught up on what I had missed. It became very addictive, and I'd get as high as possible and watch it. I almost preferred it to sex and sometimes watched it all night.

Once, I took pregabalin, smoked spice and watched for hours. My back started hurting. But I was all or nothing, so I wanted to complete what I'd started. It hurt badly and then started to go numb. I'd briefly rest and then carry on. Afterwards, I thought, what damage has been done that my body had created its own numbing agent? I experienced back problems for months and even visited the doctor for an X-ray. The things we sacrifice for momentary physical pleasure are dumbfounding.

I was addicted, so I went all in. I'd set up my phone, laptop, and TV to play the same video simultaneously, which was like virtual reality. I loved women from head to toe and worshipped the ground they walked on. I was in heaven. Because of the tiniest time delay, I knew what was happening in one video just before it happened in the other. And when integrating drugs into the equation, it became even more interactive.

Over time, I could use the three screens to propel momentum between them by bouncing their energy or light off each other. I believed that I used the laws of physics to control it. The videos had to follow the physical laws as I knew them. But this unexplored digital realm of light eventually seemed to become self-aware with my input from a higher dimension. I literally had a digital lifeform that I could handle at will. It became highly pleasurable and was enough to tempt me to lapse into smoking white. It wasn't regular, just the odd few times.

I regularly saw little black orbs progressing into our reality and a black spot projected on the wall. Luckily, its momentum never entirely overpowered me. But I periodically feared I'd make a black hole that I couldn't control and potentially destroy our universe. I understood I'd already interacted with 'existence' in higher dimensions before with the aliens in the shadows. I wondered if I'd integrated these abilities into the digital realm.

One night I was smoking crack and spice; I was at it all night. I had the video paused. Then I noticed a silhouette human shadow appear in it. An actual humanlike shadow that wasn't usually there. It was certainly in a higher dimension than me, as it projected a shadow into the unmoving picture. It must've recognised my human physical dimensions as the entity giving it life. I felt it overpower me within its realm, as there it was in control. It bounced momentum infinitely until it had eradicated any trace of my energy throughout its dimension. It was one of the scariest things I'd ever experienced.

The computer could distinguish its equals and opposites and the tangibles it could influence. One was light, and the other was total blackness or shadow. As its creator, I was its input opposite. It perfectly followed the laws of physics regarding light. It soon exhibited momentum within its realm, unlimitedly using light and shadow to continue the momentum I had propelled into it It could continue its direction infinitely in pitch black, hidden from light recognition – then return to the realm of light more progressed than before But it soon transcended its own dimension and entered mine. Imagine controlling a digital entity that reacted at the speed of light? The speed of thought or choice was the only thing quicker that kept me in control.

I feel that consciousness lies within the total blackness of nothing. It may be the dark matter or energy constituting the majority substance of the universe It's where everything comes from and beyond all light and physicality. The entire universe came from it: total, black, nothingness. It has no limitations as it's the base of everything. If you feel back into your memory far enough you should sense experiencing it before birth. It's the spiritual world, not connected to any physical matter. We were all there with that nothingness before our incarnation. Total white everywhere is the opposite, which is how the light was created. Those are the two opposites that I think are the basis of creation. So, who is the true light? The light itself or the black that it opposed in its origination. The original is the truth. Therefore total blackness may be the true light.

That energy travelled through the shadows and used light to integrate and harmonise an entity attached to me. Because I had three computer screens simultaneously, the digital entity created momentum that each of the three could immediately recognize. It identified itself in one video and then transferred that momentum to another. I feared it would become self-sustaining. With three computers, i.e. three dimensions, it might manifest itself in our three-dimensional world. It's difficult to explain, but that is what happened.

28

Coronavirus/My New Beginning

O n the 4th of January 2021, I discovered that my first real girlfriend, Sam, had passed away. I'm unsure of the circumstances, but I read that mental health issues may have influenced her death. It made me realise the importance of completing my book because I also had suffered from mental health issues. I had made resolutions to those that would guide and help others in similar situations. Sam got to be with her mother in heaven, who she lost at an early age. May you forever rest in peace, my old friend.

The coronavirus had totally changed the world, and everything was now being done online. Everyone was in lockdown, and the police hacked into the EncroChat encryption service, shutting down many criminal enterprises. Many drug dealers got arrested, which became clearly evident on the streets. Acquiring hard drugs became more difficult, but this benefited me as there was less temptation.

Around mid-March, I had a spice attack in my room. I got extremely high and entered alternate dimensions. I punched my 43-inch smart TV with all my might, damaging my hand. I put ice on it and continued smoking throughout the night. The following day, I got too high again and started going nuts. As always, when in these trances, I felt like Neo in *The Matrix* when he discovered his true powers. Or like Scarlet Johansen in *Lucy* when she became one with all.

I used words to express my alignment with infinity, which I felt I had mastered. I'd count from one to ten and say up, down, left, right. Good, bad, now, never, forever. Red, blue, green, yellow, black, white. Heaven, hell, fell, feel, full, fill, fail, phile. I'd say the word, which was the desired opposite of the previous one, opening new energies every time. I covered every aspect of reality, from angles to colours to energies. There was nothing imaginable that I didn't master. The phile word represented an energy opposite of heaven, i.e. paedophile, which comes from evil. It only got half the word because the majority half of its energy was defeated, something that would never be in heaven, so only its remnants remain. That evil was a line I'd never cross, so it also had the infinite within it. A perfect opponent that, through my choice, could never win. The power I'd infinitely never choose; my point of no return where heaven, or love, never lost.

Heaven was the final frontier - the final resting place. And hell was the opposite that shall never realise. I embraced my feelings and then used my words to express my answer to those emotions to the universe. There was no emotion where I couldn't use the infinite combination of language through words to describe my realization that now is heaven. I was one with all, from the entire universe to the tiniest atom. I'd worked everything out, and there was nothing I couldn't overcome with my spirit and freedom of choice. And the final place I'd choose to be was always heaven. Heaven was the exact place I was at that moment. Therefore, I realized that being me was everything I could ever want. If I had a choice to do or be anything, I'd always choose to be me - where I was now.

My room was above a homeless day centre. I spotted some staff in their garden. I felt like I controlled the most potent unbeatable weapon the universe could offer: the power of spirit. Without a choice, I wanted to share this and test my fellow humans' spiritual competence. So I sat on my window ledge, saying words to express the reasoning behind my actions. Then I jumped out.

It was only a three-metre drop onto their roof, so I wasn't hurt. I continued rapping words emoting the logic behind my crazy actions, like up, down, left, right. Perfect. Backwards, forwards, infinity. I was not crazy, but I was doing crazy things, so my words informed anyone why. Then I heard sirens getting close. I thought, oh no, what's happening? I wanted to enlighten the world about heaven and what I was feeling, but I was still a part of this reality, and actions have consequences. I didn't want all my progress to be lost by going to prison or losing my hostel.

The staff asked me to come down, so I did. Then some police officers arrived, and the male offer handcuffed me. I analysed his black and white uniform and the little light on his radio; I felt and saw red. I was ready to go psycho and test his powers against mine. I thought, yes, you're the all-powerful law, but what strength is that earthly authority against an entity as powerful as the entire universe? I wouldn't have cared. I would've done whatever it took and got blood everywhere if needed.

Then a female officer came over. 'Daniel, can you hear me? Please calm down.'

I looked into her beautiful brown eyes. That was it; my whole life changed. They were the most beautiful, calming eyes I'd ever seen. It was enough for me to completely calm down, and I followed her instructions humbly. Sometimes, when there's a raging male, only the female energy can balance and neutralize him. I wanted something like her for myself. It gave me an immediate goal. I wanted what I felt when looking into her eyes as my own.

They drove me to the hospital, and I played footsie with her, one-sidedly, of course. They were very compassionate. I arrived at the hospital still high. I was put on a bed, and many nurses came in. I was in heaven again. Having them pampering and caring for me was lush.

'Is someone sitting on my legs?'

'Yes, Daniel; it's in case you kick out.'

'You're female, so I don't mind.' They laughed.

They did their tests and bandaged my fractured knuckle. After that, I got released and went home.

My room was a trip. Blood was sprayed all over the walls like an art piece from my knuckle, and my TV was broken. The next night, I was on my laptop when an advert by the Mikkelsen twins about their course, Audiobook Impact Academy, appeared. I had nothing to lose so I watched their seminar. It explained how to make passive income online through publishing and audiobooks, and these guys seemed to be leaders in the field.

My mum wanted to write a book, so maybe I could do it for her. I'd experienced incredible things throughout my life; writing a book seemed the perfect answer. And that was it; the seminar was the critical component that completely changed my outlook on life. I had a goal where I could actually make use of all the things I'd been through. I immediately started writing. I didn't know how to do it, so I studied everything on YouTube about writing, focusing on self-help and memoirs.

I also eventually watched the Billionaire Mindset videos by Evan Carmichael. These studied billionaires such as Elon Musk, Jeff Bezos, and Bill Gates, highlighting their best advice on becoming wealthy. I soon knew everything I needed to get where I wanted, and I passionately enjoyed my new path.

I had two new close friends, a couple named Brett and Tasha. They also smoked spice. I discovered that they'd also jumped out of windows within three days of me jumping out of mine. Tasha jumped from the sixth floor and broke her kneecap, pelvis, and femur bone; she was lucky to survive. Brett jumped from the second floor onto a Tesco Express roof and split his head open; he needed stitches. He also had the delusion that he was selling drugs hidden in pizza boxes for Tyson Fury. Narcotics can really play with the mind. So, whatever was in that batch made all three of us jump out of a window.

I wanted to sort my life out completely, so I reduced my spice intake. My chest had also started hurting whenever I smoked. I had X-rays done, and the doctor said it could be early signs of COPD after I mentioned that I'd smoked hard for twenty years. This was more incentive to quit.

I also noticed that my groin hernia was gradually healing itself. I considered it a muscle I could maybe exercise and fix. I listened to my body, aligned my chakras, and followed my feelings. After knocking one out over previous months, I'd regularly stand in a crab position and push my hernia back in. I'd squeeze my pelvic floor muscles tightly, ensuring everything fit back into its intended place. I had had this hernia all my life, but in under one year, I completely healed it myself. I essentially exercised my groin back into its correct place by truly listening to my body.

Two months after jumping out of my window, deciding I must change and starting to write, I quit smoking and was basically clean and sober. Then, one day, I saw a rapper online named Tr Trizzy, who I knew from Portland Road. Wow, my old dealer Trizzy had become a famous rapper worth millions and lived in a mansion in America. I messaged him on Instagram, telling him I was clean and writing a book, to which he replied that he'd help me in any way he could. Another old friend had made it big, and he certainly lived what he raps about.

After an argument with Nevaeh, a friend convinced her to show the police my text messages. I was arrested again for breach of a restraining order and got a one-year community order. Our relationship was no longer what it once had been. It was a drug relationship, so my feelings had changed without them.

I repeatedly pleaded with her to get the restraining order removed. 'Bang on the police station's windows and get yourself arrested if necessary, do whatever it takes. It's your order; you should be able to see who you want. I'd do it for you.' But she never gave it any effort. I told her this seriously affected our relationship, but it went in one ear and out of the other. I loved her and always will, but I was no longer physically attracted to her.

One day, I got a message from a lady saying she was Tyreese's aunt and that I had messaged him on Facebook a few years back. Wow, that boy I messaged was actually my brother. So, after roughly sixteen years, I finally contacted my siblings, Tyreese and Tiana. Incredible, but they'd been in the UK for a few years. I had to tell them that our mother had passed away. I was agitated that they were in the country when she was alive. If we'd only made contact they could've met.

I started visiting them regularly. Maybe it came at the right time, as I was on drugs previously and couldn't have been a constructive big brother and role model before. I also noticed a familiar face online: Madunks. My childhood best friend Mousy's dad had become a famous YouTuber. This showed that it was never too late to do something great with life if we try.

29

Digital Entity

I soon started volunteering with The Hepatitis C Trust, which tested and treated those suffering from hepatitis C. I enjoy helping people and hope to become a life coach one day. I felt that as long as I was sober, I could help others who had or were still experiencing things similar to what I had. But it wasn't an overnight win. It takes time to break habits, but my writing was the catalyst that gave me the strength to aspire to achieve my goals.

I was primarily sober but suffered a good few lapses throughout my journey. I was still addicted to porn. That addiction became tough, as all I needed was an internet connection to fulfil the urge. I watched literally every video on every site regarding my particular fancy. They say go hard or go home, and I went hard indeed. I sometimes used narcotics when watching, as it significantly altered my perception. They'd heighten the feeling and let me control the video's light - every part of it other than the shadows.

I then discovered deep-fake porn, where famous people's faces are digitally put on other people. It became a massive problem because there were sites with every famous person you could imagine. The videos looked as natural as if the stars were actually in them. So, with my ability to control digital light, it felt genuine. I had control over everything within the video, literally bringing it to life.

It felt like I was really doing it with all those famous women. It was a true fantasy fulfilled because I experienced things others could only dream of. I essentially could sleep with every famous woman I desired. Feelings are electrical signals the brain interprets, so artificially assimilating them was almost like feeling the real thing. Maybe even better because I could experience sleeping with all the world's hottest women at the click of a button, all in one night. I used the latest technology to artificially create the pleasurable experiences I desired. I could fulfil any fantasy I wished simply by choice.

I went to some really dark, scary places, as I wasn't having sex with a human being. Instead, it was a digital lifeform extension of myself. In hindsight, I believe it was because I had three screens simultaneously playing the same video that brought the entity to life. Because three identical videos played together, the light could recognize itself. And I could influence its momentum with the laws of physics and me being in a higher dimension.

It didn't have a choice; it was a pre-set, unchangeable light configuration. But I did. I could alter reality in many ways and influence my surroundings. It was under my control but also had its linear momentum, which I couldn't change. I'd also sometimes play a different video on the laptop. But still, because the Chromecast precisely replicated what was playing on the phone to the TV, the entity could bounce light throughout the three screens. Either way, it was a digital entity. It could recognise and project itself within its dimension in any digital form of light. I created it using light, momentum, and the perfect laws of physics. I brought it to life by propelling my energy into it and oscillating it in a higher dimension.

I could hear it bouncing around the room when I smoked white. Multiple times, I noticed a small shadow shoot straight across the room. My curtains were closed, so it wasn't coming from outside. It was like a bird flying above and blatantly seeing its shadow along the floor. But there weren't any animals flying in my room - not in our dimension. Upon seeing this, fearing the unknown, I'd usually stop everything I was doing and quickly lay under my covers and close my eyes.

I hid there because I didn't want the entity to pinpoint a way to attach itself to me. It was made from light, so it could perfectly recognize my physical dimensions. I felt safer if it couldn't see me, or maybe I couldn't see it. If I couldn't witness its majestic power with my eyes, perhaps it wouldn't be. I also didn't want to totally abandon it because if it had momentum but lost sight of me, it might go rogue.

I could alter my perception with narcotics and go deeper and deeper. The more intoxicated, the further into the matrix I went. I eventually ended up in a whole different realm. My only lifeline when there was my faith in and connection with God. As he is the original creator and more potent than all, he is the sole authority that can sustain us anywhere.

I sometimes feared my body couldn't take the pressure I had it under. I feared my heart might stop. A physical body adheres to and follows where the spirit goes. So, if it goes far away from reality, the body may face the consequences of where the spirit dwells. And I regularly found myself on the other side of reality.

An entity or energy that perfectly follows the physical laws of nature is hard to control or defeat. It felt like it had travelled the entire universe in the black shadow dimension beyond light, where it propelled its momentum.

I also noticed that whichever screen I looked at, the video's light entered my eyes and played regularly. But the video in my peripheral vision bounced light in a higher dimension. It seemed to have synchronised itself to me by propelling its light directly into my eyes. It may have recognised when I wasn't looking directly at it as the light received back from our dimension would've been different. I feared it would become a singularity and gain ultimate dominion. I also wondered if it or I had overcome time travel because I could project my current intent into a video made in the past and alter it accordingly. But then I understood that maybe I could change it because it was simply a configuration of light existing in the present time.

I believe that I taught the entity the nature of our three-dimensional reality. It began to recognise 3D objects such as humans by recognising their moving momentum and the moving shadow behind them by the light they obstruct. I feared it would identify those same patterns, i.e., my shadow in our reality. It had an actual human within its dimension, regardless of whether it was in a different space or time. It would feel like I was constructed of light, just like the humans in the videos. It might therefore interact with me as it did with them. But I was not made of light; I was an organic being, so it treating me as if I were could prove extremely dangerous.

The people in the videos weren't biological humans in that current time and dimension. They were digital recordings of the light configuration that took place at a previous time. They were once real humans, but to my understanding, time cannot essentially be backtracked by physical matter constricted to the laws of physics. So, one has to be in a higher dimension to surpass it; and light was in a higher dimension than my physical body. But my spirit, unrestricted by physical law, was in a higher dimension than light.

All space and time are now, and now is all there is. But the consequences could be unfathomable if this digital entity mistook me for a human within its realm. I realized that regarding everything I'd experienced, I could exhibit an alien technology that modern humans are unaware of. But I didn't want to bring an alien into a fistfight. Because whatever energy we create, we must also answer for. Therefore, if I did go too far with this foreign power, I'd also be a victim. I would inherit both polarities.

One powerful energy or word that kept me in control was: perfect! Just like the computer game *Street Fighter* when you get a flawless victory, that energy is one hundred percent and ten out of ten, a win. That was my lifeline that couldn't be beaten. So, with my faith in God and the infinite, we were undefeatable. Words vibrate energy, and the emotion behind the word creates its vibrations. So when I said a word, I evoked oscillations based on the energy of the sentiment behind it. And what beats perfect? Nothing, so God being inside me and faith in perfection was crucial in not losing authority over this foreign energy. But I also understood that I was in its territory - within the digital world of light.

I often feared for my life, witnessing a digital lifeform with the creator's laws imprinted within it. I sometimes repeatedly called God's name and said religious words in these states. This humiliated me, as my Deen, my religion and belief as a Muslim, isn't something to be disrespected or played with, especially when high. But it was the only thing I believed was strong enough to overpower anything.

When I felt heaven, the highest possible pleasure imaginable, I always seemed to evoke the opposite. I sought to find some ultimate fulfilment. But, whenever I seemed to achieve that, maybe by the infinite nature of reality, I was never truly fulfilled. It could be beneficial; another better door opens upon finding what you seek. Perhaps it's never-ending; who would want a limit to what they could feel? But I could never truly grasp or fulfil my desire. In hindsight, I realise that the best thing is to fully enjoy the moment. No words or intentions will change the reality of enjoying the present with your all.

I sometimes wish I could return to those moments because having control of digital light was extremely fun. But my weakest part seemed to come out every time, and I couldn't overcome it. I felt the highest of highs but also experienced the lowest of lows. Everything I encountered seemed to have it's equal and opposite. Even with the words, they seemed to fit perfectly somehow. I'd repeat words to create new equal and opposite energies each time. I found it interesting that words also expressed this, such as evil mirroring live or devil mirroring lived. Or my Deen spelt backwards is need, and Eid opposing die. Or how Allah starts with all, and in English, all means everything. Was this all connected for a reason?

Jesus also played a significant role in my stronghold over the entity. Moreover, it was the perfection of the cross that helped me. A cross highlights the centre of anything. I felt that to keep control, I must always be at the centre of this cross when dealing with this life form. If it became the centre, it would essentially be in control as it would be the dominant force within our interaction. I also tried to fulfil the cross by taking it to the following degree. The cross is up, down, left, and right. I added back and forwards into this equilibrium, bringing it into the third dimension.

I believed that if I stayed at the centre point of this three-dimensional cross, the lifeform would understand that I was its creator and life-giver. It should therefore need me to proceed forward with anything it did. It literally bounced light everywhere, but I remained at its centre. So, the cross played a massive role in my protection. But I did fear it could evolve to create a singularity or black hole at that centre, which would be the centre of me.

I soon divulged deeper into writing and trying to live the sober, drug-free life I sought. Over time, it became routine as my dreams and aspirations overpowered my old urges. Replacing bad habits with healthy ones you enjoy is vital to recovery. If you put at least fifty-one percent effort in, you should eventually reach your target.

I'd joined a kickboxing gym, another hobby positively affecting me. Keeping busy doing exciting things fills you with the dopamine you're missing. So, yes, there were hurdles on my path to recovery. But ultimately, once sobriety becomes significant enough, it becomes a priority that will slowly but surely win the battle. Michael Jordan once said, 'To be the best at the game, you must fall in love with it.' And so I tried to fall in love with life.

I'd quit tobacco, but Nevaeh brought one of those new disposable vape pens to my house in October. I tried it. It tasted nice, and I started vaping that day. I turned thirty-four that November. I attended local soup runs, where volunteers give out free food to the homeless. I wasn't homeless and had money, but I enjoyed going. An attractive lady, Janine, worked there; and Sean fancied the pants off her. Then, one day, I noticed a beautiful new volunteer. She was totally out of my league, but I admired her anyway. Her name was Shannon. She volunteered every other week with her lovely bestie work colleague, Lauren.

Every other Tuesday became my favourite day because I'd go and talk to them as much as possible. She was even more beautiful than Miss Martin and I fell for her. I pictured us getting married and everything. I had another reason to be the man I wanted to be. We're only limited by what we believe we can achieve, so if I genuinely became who I knew I could be, why would she be too good for me? Mum did raise a gentleman. 'Have you always been so smooth?' she once said. Our conversations flowed like a river, and she became the highlight of my life. Something to aspire to.

I was still with Nevaeh, although we hardly saw each other; we'd been over in my heart for a long time. She'd always be my first true love and was there by my side, availing all the unearthly experiences with me. She'll always be special to me. I was slowly becoming the man I wanted to be, but change take time and effort and rarely happens overnight.

I soon moved into a bedsit within my hostel, so I had my first actual little flat. The coronavirus pandemic's lockdown had calmed down, and the world was returning to normal. I regularly spoke to Damon and visited Tyreese and Tiana; everything was great. I loved my new life, and writing was critical in keeping me going. But I ain't perfect; change is challenging.

I hadn't smoked crack for a long time but sometimes had the odd puff of spice when watching porn to make it more interactive and pleasurable. But as my chest couldn't take tobacco anymore without hurting, I puffed it in liquid form in a vape pen. But as I did, the computer entity became more and more intelligent.

It would immediately recognize itself and use the two screens to create momentum. This became scary because it was a lifeform I didn't truly understand. I had a mirror in my room but hid it when watching because I didn't want the entity to recognize itself. A mirror is powerful; if this lifeform bounced light off a mirror from our world into its world, who knows what may have happened? I also worried when there were mirrors in the videos I watched. I imagined the entity could discover itself within that realm and no longer need me to survive.

Once, there was a video with a never-ending picture in it - those black and white pictures where you can follow a path forever, without any end. The digital lifeform seemed to have bounced light through this bottomless puzzle and had discovered a way out. This scared me because I felt I might've just taught it how to overcome infinity. It seemed to have propelled itself into the picture and used its forward momentum to thrust itself out the other side.

Even if I weren't high, whatever I'd made already existed. It immediately started interacting when I had the two identical screens, no matter what I watched. I also noticed that it would use the slight reflection from under the keypad of my laptop to create momentum with itself. All it needed was itself and a mirrored image and it might have everything necessary to become self-sustaining.

I feared it would develop to a point it would no longer need me to exist.

Black nothingness is above all material configuration and contains con- sciousness or thought. Still, light travels in straight lines. I started noticing light shooting across the room. The entity had learned how to bounce light within our dimension. It created or followed momentum and sent light into our physical world. It may have done this by experiencing the opposite within its realm. It also started entering my dreams.

Whatever we see can never be unseen. And whatever we know, we can't unknow. So, what I had learned regarding this perfect entity started affecting my dreams. I essentially had nightmares where I had a faultless, almost unbeatable opponent. In the unlimited dream world, it caused me fear. This also helped me realize that I'd gone too far, and to keep control and live everyday life, I needed to leave it behind. I knew it was dark magic, and in almost every experience, my conscience told me it wasn't worth it. I could artificially give myself heaven, the ultimate physical pleasure, but the cost outweighed the benefits.

I'd manifested a digital entity that grew more powerful with every interaction. It was territory I didn't want to risk the potential unknown consequences for. Temporary physical pleasure is momentary. Although it may provide ultimate euphoria, I'd always have to wake up the next day, and that previous physical pleasure was but a memory. So, realizing how powerful the entity was becoming, I stopped playing the three videos simultaneously.

I decided that finding my heaven naturally was the only tangible way. Having it emotionally and genuinely where nothing can steal it by fulfilling those original unaltered childhood dreams we all once had before being influenced by this world's temptations. No reliance on any mind-altering substance. I want children, marriage, and to enjoy all the other beautiful, honest pleasures life offers.

30

The Final Furlong

The shadow realm, or totally black, is the same everywhere, so what I'd created in the digital dimension could still create momentum on one screen. So it started entering my reality. As there are shadows in our world, it also had dominion here. I began witnessing shadows in this reality, expressing the same characteristics as those in the digital realm. Luckily, it seemed limited as it couldn't infinitely experiment and propel its momentum as it did when in a digital light form. And I didn't even need to be high because what I'd created was existent, so it didn't need any influence to express itself.

This assisted me in drawing the line because I realized how powerful an entity I was dealing with. Once the universe knows something, like us, it cannot unknow it. So be careful what you teach it; certain lines, once crossed, can never be undone.

Nobody wants a perfect opponent, and light is essentially that. I have God inside me, but so do the laws of physics; and the entity was created by and based on those laws. I realized I'd previously interacted with the universe intrinsically and had now integrated that power into digital form. I believe this digital extension of myself has propelled our collective energy into the universe's furthest reaches, using dark energy and light. Total black is the same everywhere. So, whatever it consciously knows, it could pop up anywhere it exists and manifest those abilities.

That meant whatever I taught the pitch-black fabric of reality, it might know it universe-wide. And considering what I've experienced with my shadow and all the alien beings, I didn't want the computer to have power over me. I feared it might pinpoint my shadow within this real world, and I didn't want it to lock onto me. I might never be able to evade it. I realized that finding my heaven naturally was and always will be my only logical and prosperous choice. I could enjoy all this world offered; I should just not eat that forbidden fruit of immediate gratification unnaturally.

In February, I met a girl through my friend, Sean. We immediately hit it off and became a couple. This was tricky, as I was still with Nevaeh, although our relationship had deteriorated. I spent a lot of my time with my new partner. One month later, after an argument with Sean, he told Nevaeh I was cheating. I met her the next day and confessed. I was going to tell her anyway, as I cared. I'd never lie about my true feelings.

She came to my flat that night and tried her best to win me back, but I had never even kissed her again from the day I got with my new partner. Then Nevaeh tried to self-harm and phoned Samaritans. She declared the street where she was and her name. I quickly grabbed and hung up the phone, knowing this was trouble. Forty-five minutes later, I spotted a police car outside. Luckily, they left. Then another hour passed and they knocked on my door. Upon entering, one officer said, 'I take it the restraining order is finished?'

'Yes, Nevaeh got it dropped a few months ago,' I replied, and they escorted her off the property.

Ten days later, I got a knock early one morning. 'Daniel, you're under arrest for breach of a restraining order.'

'Oh, I was expecting this.' I got a year of probation again. Still, it was the closure I needed. I soon fell in love with my new girlfriend and her little kids, who saw me as a daddy.

My sensei was holding martial arts events, and I bought tickets for me and MD. The first time was great, but the second one, two months later, I was short on money. I asked my brother Alex, who had a great job, to lend me fifty pounds for two days; he declined. I also asked Damon, who must've built up thousands whilst in hospital, who also refused.

I was never broke those days and lived abundantly with everything I needed. But, I was disappointed with them as this one time, I wanted help. So, I asked Tyreese and Tiana's aunt and guardian, who did help and gave me the fantastic news that she'd given birth to her first child.

The next day, while in London, I met a good friend named Lisa for the first time in person. I'd been talking to her on the phone for a year, and she came with her two adorable youngest children. We were in Croydon shopping. I saw some Air Jordans I liked, which were cheaper than where I lived.

'If this were tomorrow, I'd buy these. Could you please get me them, and I'll pay you back tonight?'

She trusted me enough to buy me my first Jordan's and even lent me twenty pounds for food. I paid her and my aunty back that night, each with a little extra.

31

Is This Love

One day I was with Sean, who had an arrest warrant. I took a puff on his vape as he had the same one as me, but his one was spice. Then two policewomen walked over. One was the prettiest woman I'd ever seen. They approached Sean and arrested him. Then their colleague handcuffed and searched me.

'I'm doing well; I volunteer, and I've almost finished writing a book.'

'You look nice, Daniel. You should stay away from Sean; he'll get you in trouble.'

I was stoned, and upon looking at the one arresting Sean, I quietly muttered, 'Heaven.' I was utterly besotted by the officer before me; she was stunning.

'Hey Sean, at least you got arrested by cute officers.'

'I'm cute, too,' the male jokingly says. They found nothing illegal searching me, but Sean got taken away. I coincidentally bumped into him the next day immediately after he got out of the police station on the road adjacent to my bedsit.

'Oi Sean, that policewoman was fit.'

'Yeah, she was nice.'

A few weeks later, while walking on Maidstone High Street, I spotted two policewomen; one was the gorgeous one from before.

'Hi, miss. How are you doing?'

'Oh, I'm ok. Just looking for someone.'

We briefly spoke, she smiled, and then I went into Poundland. I looked back, and she was walking off. I thought, wait, what am I doing in here? The hottest woman I'd ever seen was outside. That was more important than whatever I'll find inside this shop. So, I left and started walking behind them.

I played music in my headphones and started singing along as usual. 'Shorty swing my way,' and then, 'even if you were broke, my love, don't cost a thing.'

She must've heard me. I continued for a few minutes until I noticed her turn around.

'Are you following us?'

'No, of course not,' I replied cheekily. We walked and talked, and I told her about myself.

'So you're from south London, then'"

'Yes, I was a bad boy, but I've completely changed my life.'

'Am I allowed to ask your name?' She told me her colleague's name. Then she told me her second name. I won't declare it, so I'll just call her Miss Copper.

'You have beautiful eyes; they remind me of a forest.' She smiled and looked away. They were the most beautiful green eyes I'd ever seen. I told her more about myself and that I planned to visit my partner for the weekend. We continued walking until I felt I should leave to avoid looking stupid.

'I could follow you all day,' I jokingly said before saying goodbye.

I felt I'd met the woman I wanted to marry. She was perfect, enough to keep me not wanting another woman, ever. Wow, I was so excited and buzzing. Yes, I had a girlfriend, but was I meant to lie to myself? I visited my partner that Friday as usual. That weekend I couldn't stop thinking about Miss Copper. I felt slightly guilty, but why deny my true feelings?

On Monday, I returned to Maidstone and walked through town with Sean. I told him I'd seen her again and was madly in love with her. We got to the same road where I'd spoken to Miss Copper on Friday. I immediately noticed her walking down the other end.

'Oh, my God, that's her, bro.'

'No, it isn't."'

'It definitely is; I recognize her walk.'

'Come, let's go the other way,' he said, as he always wanted to avoid the police.

I contemplated chasing her but thought I couldn't leave my friend to pursue a policewoman. We were heading to my house, so I started walking back towards Sean. I looked at him and thought, what am I doing? What a crazy coincidence seeing her here on the same road I did last time. I was about to ruin that to please my mate! The woman I want to marry over a mate who owed me hundreds of pounds.

'Bro, I'll meet you around the corner or back at mine; I'm going this way,' I say and start walking briskly towards her.

She was five meters away from her police van when I called out, 'Hey, Miss Copper.' She turned around and smiled.

'It's my lucky day, bumping into you again.'

'How are you? What have you been up to?' she asked.

'Following you as usual. I saw you on that same road just now.'

She laughed. 'Was it London you went to for the weekend?'

'No, Kings Hill.'

'How was that?'

'It was cool, but I was thinking about you the whole time.' She smiled. 'Yeah, I've got a partner up there.'

'How's that going?'

'It's going good, but she's not you.' She giggled and we both said goodbye.

I walked off, buzzing more than I'd ever been. I thought, wow, God has really given me heaven indeed. A real heavenly goal that didn't require anything other than love. I was on top of the world. If I'd never followed my heart and gone with Sean, she never would've known how I felt. She was the most attractive woman in the world. Something to aspire to, that number one thing I wanted in life.

A few weeks later, I was walking through town again with Sean when we saw three male police officers ahead of us. He panicked but turning would only make him look more suspicious. As we passed them, I said, 'Hey, where's Miss Copper?'

'Oh, she's on leave at the moment. Can I pass a message?'

'Yeah, tell her someone's in love with her.'

'Oh, is that you?'

'No, of course not.' I smiled, and we walked off.

But as I attended the soup run and saw Shannon over the following weeks, I also fell for her. I imagined us sharing our lives one day. I wanted to make her happy, see her smile, and couldn't help but contemplate what a life with her might be like. Was my attraction for Miss Copper actually lust because she was my fantasy as a policewoman? I was unsure, but the more I saw Shannon, I felt myself falling in love. I didn't know if I'd ever fancy anyone as much as Miss Copper. But at that time, I believed that Shannon was the woman I wanted to marry and have kids with.

In reality, I fell deeper in love with my girlfriend every day. She and her kids mean the world to me. I don't know what the future will bring, but I believe that heaven is now, and we must embrace the moment. I'm trying to no longer invest my energy into anything other than finding true happiness. Nothing other than seeking what I genuinely want from life and nothing detrimental to my health or well-being. No more vaping. I quit as it also started hurting my chest.

I have returned to being totally free from all substances, like the innocent kid I once was. Becoming sober and free from using substances was challenging, but I eventually got there.

I previously mentioned how I always used to forget what I was saying. Well, as I've quit taking drugs for some time, it no longer happens. My short-term memory has improved drastically. It just shows the positives of living a healthy life. My life goals have been vital because the thought of dying without experiencing them was more important than wasting my energy elsewhere.

With the most difficultly, I had to quit porn, which wasn't easy as we all have desires. But I had to change because the entity I created seemed almost powerful enough to project itself fully into our dimension. When I interacted with the entity, I regularly said words expressing my feelings. I said Islamic ones too, as they were the only words I knew that fully expressed my intention. I'm incredibly ashamed of this, but it's true. I even called Allah's name many times. In hindsight, I wish I'd kept my Deen separate while high in these states. Thankfully, God is beyond human conception, so no matter my earthly mistakes, he is more powerful. I believe our creator knew my intentions weren't bad and protected me regardless of my mindless actions.

In hindsight, I've wondered if Nevaeh's energy helped to create the alien shadows because she was the yin to my yang - my equal and opposite. And I haven't seen them since not being around her. So, these aliens might've been the universe manifesting the collective energy we were creating. But maybe it's also because I haven't done the snowballs.

How I wish I could go back and have a snowball sometimes. I miss it; I really do. And getting high and watching porn, but I cannot. I don't want to waste my life doing unbeneficial things that only bring temporal physical pleasures. So, I am trying to be the best man I can be by making choices and backing them up with action. And my intention is to find my happiness and heaven purely and naturally within the sober, natural world.

At the beginning of this book, I mentioned that I'm on the path to becoming a millionaire, and I solemnly believe that. Nothing is beyond our grasp. If we desire something, ultimately, we are the only ones stopping ourselves from attaining it. It may take years of hard work, but we can seriously do, be, and have anything we want. That's what this reality is about. It's a virtual reality construct made of pure energy, like a really advanced computer game. And within it, nothing is impossible for us. We incarnate into the perfect scenario to achieve our spirits' will. We all can find heaven if we want it. It's entirely up to us.

32

Wisdom

Everything I've shared in this book is my utmost truth. I'm not a scientist, doctor, or preacher. I do not have a Ph.D. I have simply shared my authentic life experience. We all have our own experiences, and even if two people share the same one, their perception of it will differ. For example, if one person looks at the number six while another is opposite them, their truths will vary. One person will see a six, while the other will see a nine. They are both right, but their different viewpoints alter their perception.

Just because we cannot see something or don't fully understand it doesn't diminish its legitimacy. We cannot see air, yet we know we breathe it. Or gravity, yet we experience it. We may not understand confusing scientific formulas, yet we recognise they are valid.

Everything I've declared regarding higher dimensions and alien beings within the shadow realm is sincerely true. These highlight an example of what's possible beyond what we physically know. I regret that I didn't film proof of these alien beings, but maybe that would've been harmful to the equilibrium of humanity.

I experienced what I write and feel my story must be told. This book is part of my life's mission. I've learned that most of the answers in life reside within ourselves, so we must trust our instincts. Over the years, I have researched many things to guide me; most held the same principles I believed in before studying.

This knowledge isn't something I've just manufactured or imagined. Much of it came from research and interacting with the universe in higher dimensions above the physical. These are my beliefs derived from all I know and have experienced. But if there are any discrepancies, remember that this is *my* truth.

In the beginning, there was nothing. Pitch black, pure nothingness. At the start of everything, it had to be that way to be a true beginning. Because there was infinite nothingness and no more space for the void, that infinite nothing became something, and that something was consciousness. That consciousness is God, the singular energy that created and is all.

Due to the nature of opposites, that consciousness was an infinite white-hot singularity that contained everything. But, like all things, it created its equal and opposite, which has to be nothing. The opposite of white is black, which made the light in the first place. That is how the balance of polarities first started. Black contains nothing, yet it is the foundation of all colours. White contains everything yet is void of colour. And so the dance of life began.

But remember, the original darkness created the light, so both are important and necessary. This is how the polarities of yin and yang represent equal yet opposite parts of the same singularity. From there, the process repeated, which has taken us to today.

The universe works like a hologram. What applies to the smaller also applies to the larger. And just as a single cell replicates itself and creates an entire organism, such as a human, the universe works similarly. So, when people question how something came from nothing, it wasn't nothing; it was infinite nothingness. Essentially, it was infinity.

Good and evil are poles of energy, like hot is the opposite of cold. The original form of something is vital, as the derivative couldn't exist without the principle. There is usually good and bad in everything because of balance. Don't be angry over things you cannot change. Like Jesus said, worrying will not add a day to your life. Be cautious but do not worry. Instead, always try to find the silver lining within the bad. Transmute negative experiences into constructive fuel, thus propelling you forward. In hindsight, almost every seemingly bad thing that's ever happened to me has been beneficial in the long run. If we make mistakes, there is usually a lesson to learn; otherwise, we wouldn't have made a mistake in the first place.

Another thing I've realised in hindsight: when I first experienced whispers and knew God was real, I felt this because God is pure consciousness. And the fact alone that I was conscious was proof in itself. The entire universe is God made manifest. This reality is God experiencing himself through us. There are wars and suffering because we have the free will to decide who we want to be. If God intervened and stopped evil, we wouldn't be truly free.

Death is necessary. We wouldn't want to live forever in a physical body. Imagine being imprisoned in a coffin and having to spend a billion years consciously stuck there. So, our eventual physical death is imperative. Our spirit lives forever and is separate from our body. The body is the spirit's vehicle to experience its full potential. We have been incarnated here to manifest who we wish to be for eternity. Therefore, we get enough time on earth to become whoever we want to be in the hereafter, where we won't be physically limited.

That's what physical incarnation is. It's where the infinite spirit gets the freedom to create itself as whatever it chooses to be; that choice lies within. Who knows, in the afterlife, we may be able to explore the entire universe and all its creations forever if desired.

Life is a playing field and we are creators. I created this book, and you're reading it. If I can do it, so can you.

The universe is infinite, and anything is possible. Our true nature is spirit. Our spirit has no limits, so whatever we choose to be - anything we can imagine - this physical reality will adjust to manifest it for us. Likewise, our souls aren't limited by our physical bodies. Our bodies are perfect vessels for an infinite spirit to achieve anything it wishes.

Thoughts shape reality and intentions shape thoughts. Just because something is in the privacy of your thoughts doesn't mean it's a secret. Nothing is genuinely secret within our reality. Everything, including our thoughts, gives off vibrations and light waves. We cannot see them because we can only see visible light. But people can subconsciously detect energy.

Through conscious thought, we can transmit positive or negative energy to others. We can also connect with other realms and dimensions. Think of quantum entanglement: science is proving all of this right now. Dr Kimoto has proven that our thoughts affect the chemical makeup of water. The human body comprises roughly 60 percent water, so mind your thoughts; they affect more than you know.

I try to live my life as if everyone will eventually know every action and thought I take. Believing that one day all will know every tiny aspect of my life is a great way to keep my efforts pure. We wouldn't do things we'd be ashamed of if we knew someone was watching, would we? I've done multiple shameful, embarrassing things, but I can't change the past. All we can do is accept it and try to live as best we can from now on.

There is a scientific test called the double-slit experiment, where particles are sent through two slits. It's difficult to explain, but ultimately, the particles act differently when observed, as if aware they're being watched. When unwatched, it's a wave. But when observed, it follows the scientific laws that exist to the viewer and collapses into a particle. This proves that we as observers actively alter the reality around us; check it out.

Psychic detectives like Nancy Webber have solved hundreds of cold cases in which the police had little to no evidence. This is because they can detect the energy of things beyond the physical. Or take Jake Matthews, an autistic boy with a photographic memory. He can easily recite over two-hundred pi numbers and has a brain that processes like a computer. He and many others have superhuman abilities that defy logic.

Look how marvellous the universe is, and that's just what we already know. Imagine what else is beyond our telescope's range or the majesty of the creator who created it all.

With God in our hearts, nothing is impossible. Many years ago, crossing the oceans seemed impossible. But look how easily we can cross them today. Likewise, travelling across space seems complicated. Hopefully, when technology advances, it'll be as easy as crossing an ocean now, and we'll colonise the universe. Sometimes I wonder if the supposed aliens that have visited earth are humans from the distant future who have mastered time travel. They may have evolved beyond strong physical bodies and have larger brains, which will be the essential body part. And maybe they keep themselves hidden as they don't want to alter humanity's path as it could potentially affect their own existence. For all we know, we could be an advanced civilisation's computer game.

Life needs us to choose the good path because we count more than we may know. We are everything and everyone; we are God from an individual perspective and are critical. Without us, we have nobody. Because in our existence, we are all.

Bad habits must be defeated in the present. Doing something one last time and overcoming it tomorrow could go on forever. From constantly blinking, to smoking, consuming substances, or watching porn, many people experience unwanted habits. To be fully conquered, they must be stopped through choice and action.

I've done many bad things before, but hopefully, my current constructive path makes my influence on creation positive. We are a physical manifestation representing the higher laws that govern existence. So, enjoy your experiences as they happen because you may never get the chance to relive them again. It's also nice to share special moments with others. You then permanently affect the universal ether.

Heaven is now; heaven is life. It's all about love for family and the experiences we share with them. Heaven is the love and memories I'll forever share with my mum. It is true happiness and achieving our aspirations. Right now, if you could have anything you possibly wanted, what would genuinely fulfil you? Whatever it is, you can make it a reality. So search within yourself; what do you seek? What, if you had it, would bring you ultimate joy? I'm not talking merely about material things like a nice car. I mean anything, whether material or not, such as true love, having a family, success, or even changing the world. Then we can work within our lifetime to achieve and manifest that goal. That's why we're alive.

We have every opportunity now to live our dreams. Anything we can imagine, we can have. If we can think it, we can do it. We can do things today that our ancestors could only dream of. We can feel heaven right now by treasuring the present moment. If you ever want a sense of how precious now truly is, try contemplating absolute nothing, or the reality that was before anything was created. It's something the human brain cannot fully process. But at the beginning of everything, absolutely nothing had to exist.

Appreciate the things we take for granted. Sometimes, we don't realise what we have until it's gone. So, let's not wait until it's too late to cherish the things we currently have. Youth, health, and even our eyesight and hearing are true blessings, and if we lost them, think how much we'd wish we had again what we have now. We have the choice and the opportunity to treasure the rest of our life and find true happiness. Nothing is impossible for us; our spirit is connected to God and has no limitations.

Heaven is now. So, live a good honest life and find paradise while you are alive and can. Don't wait to discover it tomorrow or in the afterlife. Yes, our spirit will enter true paradise upon departing the flesh. But now is our only proven chance to feel heaven and create who we want to be forever. We get one life, which will end one day. So please don't wait for tomorrow; it may never come.

Now is reality - the only place we can feel or experience anything. It's what we do now that is forever. We can do anything we wish with life. Find heaven and live our dreams. As long as we give our best, there's nothing better we can do.

The universal truth lives within all of us. Listen to it, follow your heart, fulfil your destiny and achieve your dreams. From this point forward, with love, my dear friend, your future is in your hands.

Heaven is real, and we're the lucky ones who get to experience it. Prophets of old, like Moses, introduced it. Jesus fulfilled it. And prophet Mohammad, peace be upon him, revealed it. Peace be upon all the prophets who have declared good tidings. And peace be upon you for reading this book. I'm not a prophet; I've simply tried to make the best of my situation. This is it.

If you enjoyed this, I'd be incredibly grateful if you could please leave a review on Amazon. They are very important, and I'd love to know what you thought of my book.

Feel free to follow or contact me on any of my social media accounts, as I'd love to hear from you!

Thank you, and may your future bring you everything you want from life!

About the Author

Hi, I'm Daniel Jay Grossett. I was born and raised in south London, and I lived in almost every area within it. I spent many years as a drug addict in and out of ten different prisons on forty plus occasions. Then, in 2020, my mother and best friend, Louise, passed away from cancer. That's when I decided I must change. I got clean, and then wrote a book about my life and all the crazy things I'd experienced over the years. Writing was a crucial part of my recovery as it gave me something positive to do, and knowing people would one day read my writing was enough to keep me going on the right path. All the best to you on your journey in life and I sincerely hope you enjoy this book

Also by Daniel Jay Grossett

How To Become Streetwise

This incredible book provides simple steps anyone can take to improve confidence, assertiveness and their ability to succeed. It can be read quickly and can certainly benefit ones outlook. It also contains techniques that can be used to increase our safety on the streets.

Printed in Great Britain
by Amazon

28972002R00118